stoned, naked, and looking in my neighbor's window

stoned, naked, and looking in my neighbor's window

the best confessions from grouphug.us

compiled by Gabriel Jeffrey
creator of grouphug.us

justin, charles, & company
boston, massachusetts

Every effort has been made to fulfill requirements with regard to reproducing copyright material. The author and publisher will be glad to rectify any omissions at the earliest opportunity.

ISBN: 1-932112-36-7

Library of Congress Cataloging-in-Publication Data is available.

Published in the United States by Justin, Charles & Co., Publishers, 20 Park Plaza,
Boston, MA 02116
www.justincharlesbooks.com

Distributed by National Book Network, Lanham, Maryland
www.nbnbooks.com

10 9 8 7 6 5 4 3 2 1

Printed in the United States of America

For my Mom and Dad,
for telling me they're proud
even through clenched teeth.

I would like to thank Robert Cope and Adam Bregenzer for their technical might and generosity.

In the first weeks online, when I was completely unprepared for the flood of confessions, my brother Logan spent hours removing the junk submissions.

My special girl, Leah, inspires me and keeps me grounded.

I would also like to thank Yimay Yang, Honor, Max, the moderators of Group Hug, Bosey Masket, and, of course, the thousands of people who have told me their private stories.

contents

stoned, naked, and looking in my neighbor's window

confession

"Their beauty is their confession."
— ST. AUGUSTINE

This is a book of confessions from the Internet, the Shangri-La of anonymous, voyeuristic gratification. In it you will read things that revolt you on the same page as things that you'll wish to hell you were young/limber/stupid enough to try.

Grouphug.us is a Web site where anyone can confess anything anonymously. You type your confession, click a button, and a jillion people read it. The idea is that it's sort of soothing to let your skeletons peek out of the closet. It's pages were seen more than 13 million times in the first three months of its existence. A proper meme, it spread without advertising or — really — any effort at all. It all started as a spontaneous social experiment born of a drunken father on a Tuesday night. It was named on September 29, 2003, partly thanks to iChat and a very important conversation with my friend Yimay:

12:05 AM
Me: Should my confession site be grouphug.us?
Her: Ha-ha. Yes.
Me: Really?
Her: Yes. I like it. What else you got.
Me: I've been looking for .us domains 'cause they're silly and cheap.

> Her: How cheap?
> Me: $5
> Her: Wow!
> Me: Maybe I'll stay up and build the site! I can't sleep anyway.
> Her: Do it!

12:10 AM

> Me: I bought grouphug.us.
> Her: Yay.
> Me: How silly . . . ok, I'm going to get a snack, then group therapy building.
> Her: I'm having water for snack.
> Me: You have to make up some confessions. I decided that it has to be totally confidential. No email address or anything 'cause otherwise my friends won't trust it.
> Her: 'Cause I'm sick, and have no appetite really.

Yimay and I have a special bond. She's Chinese and I tend to consider myself at least partly Chinese, what with three adopted Chinese cousins and all.

I've tried on a few answers to Why did you do this? and they all fit a little differently. For the full story, you have to look at the cultural history of the Web. Not as technology, but as a medium. You also have to understand that everything I say here is completely true because it's in a book.

It's not porno, Nigerian bank scams, junk mail, viruses, bad design, and sexy pinups of Rob Reiner[1] that's sucking the fun out of the Internet. It's the same party of ugly rich fatties that at one time or another tries to ruin everything good. The Web as we know it is about 14 years old[2];

1. Swear to God, my girlfriend was looking at these last night.

2. In 1990 Tim Berners-Lee created the first graphical Web browser, "WorldWideWeb."

a young, fresh-faced thing still finding her place in the world. The average American CEO is a man in his fifties. In Canada and countries that speak Spanish or end in "ania" this is a legal, if frowned upon, congress. But as the Internet's primary residence is still the States, and the bald, Viagra-jacked captains of industry generally ~~pay taxes~~ have most of their houses here as well, it's a tragedy to see the sparkle, the *joie de vive,* leaving Webigail's eyes as the ham-fisted, greedy perves look for every possible way to exploit everything with value and destroy anything that threatens their dominance.

The first phase of the World Wide Web was sort of like a big record convention. If you were there then you knew everyone already. There were side deals and pissing contents but everyone was on the same side, working to create something. We'll call this the '70s and '80s. (This is a gross oversimplification, and I will get angry email from my many powerless critics.) Through the '90s the Internet started to look a lot more like Tijuana. There were lots of stories about the crazy shit that went on but when you got there it was hard to figure out what to do. A merchant lured you in with the promise that the first lap dance is free but after being sat on by a pregnant eighteen year old and somehow spending $80 on a couple of warm Corona's, you start to think about the old "Free Lunch" axiom. A few customers lost their shirts; a few bartenders gave away the house. When the coke wore off and the fog of the post-boom hangover started to lift, there were a few companies left over: the *maquiladoras.* Brick-and-mortar businesses selling the same old products you get back on the other side of the border for a lot less. CFO Rich Dickpants may have been entertaining underage boys the night before, but by noon he was straightening his tie and he knew who to blame for all the trouble: everyone else. The Internet was too consumer-friendly. There was free product. Free news, free entertainment, free information, free communication. It was time to litigate. There are now patents on clicking your mouse button once, clicking your mouse button twice (different companies), entertaining cats with flashlights, displaying advertisements, pausing video, and sending greeting cards. Microsoft has a patent on a particular variety of apple tree. Companies were suing each other left and right because the modern company has a fiduciary responsibility to not be responsible for their own failure. This doctrine was taken to a new low with the still-widening practice of suing your own customers. Contracts written to become effective when you opened a software box were placed inside the box. The Recording Industry of America[3] released even less of the god-awful crap music than they usually do and blamed financial losses on customers *not buying enough music.* So they sued a twelve-year-old girl. Manufacturers of various devices even got in the habit of suing customers for making the stuff that they bought work better.

The Internet companies that did manage to survive the overblown tech bust consolidated like mad. They stopped inventing cool shit and before long 75 percent of the Internet looked the same.

And that's when the creepy office party started.

If you were in your twenties in 2003, then chances are pretty good you know someone who updated their Friendster[4] profile every day for at least a week: the week that Friendster (and all of the clones) was interesting. So you wind up with a blog[5] to show how introspective you are, your Friendster profile to show how interesting and popular you are, and your new chinos from the GAP (wrinkle free) to show how stylish (and sensible) you are.

3. riaa.org.
4. friendster.com.
5. Shortened form of Web log: a series of frequently boring and almost always narcissistic rants.

So this is the new Internet. It's an office party, maybe an after-work happy hour in the cafeteria with free Heineken and jalapeño poppers. Everybody looks oh-so-put-together in knitwear and haircuts they saw in *Rolling Stone* and if your numbers look good enough this quarter you might get that 2 percent raise you've been jonesing so hard for. Maybe you can finally get that Miata you've been eyeing, finally ask the boss's assistant out to Chili's, or something. Finally get a handjob maybe. Sky's the limit!

Then you remember that the best experiences of your life are the ones where you're not a customer. When there is no product, no value-proposition. Swimming in the ocean. Eating berries from a vine. Screwing without a condom.

It was these sentiments, and the inevitability of their cooption by Diesel and Volkswagen, that got me thinking about a new project. The heart of it would be anonymity, which is terribly undervalued. If you're at a party giving out business cards, nobody's writing songs about you. Go to a rock show and buy drinks for strangers, they'll remember you. People tell better stories to strangers.

When it came to the context and the format, it seemed sort of obvious. Confession — whether once a week in a booth to a priest, or once a week in a civic building to a bunch of fellow alcoholics — has this sacred, candid, alarmingly visceral meaning to a lot of people. Calling these anonymous stories confessions would require very little further explanation. I wanted to collect stories about weakness, rage, affairs, desperation, fetishes, and all the other really human things that don't belong on an earnings report. The truth is that most jobs suck, being fat and spoiled doesn't make kids happy, your girlfriend might have been thinking about someone else last night, the kid at the burger place probably *will* spit in your food if you're a dick to him.

So on October 1, 2003 I posted the first confession, a simple one:

469666749

I normally do not smoke, but when I am really stressed out about something I can comfortably smoke nearly a pack a day.

And posted a link on my blog.[6]

For the first several days it was an intimate little site that only a few people knew about; a big game of truth or dare with a few friends out on the small back porch of my apartment. That metaphor got flimsy in the second week and by week three the porch would have caved in, killing and maiming hundreds — there were more than 2.5 million pages served up that week.

I designed and built that first version of the site in a matter of four hours. It was not designed with scale in mind. That month I recruited my brother, Logan, to help plow through the confessions. My mom offered, but I felt a little protective of her. The number of visitors and new confessions was growing like . . . something that grows really fast which meant that I needed to quickly develop a new version of the software that ran grouphug.us. I put out the call for overqualified developers (who were dying to work for free on a thankless project) to send me samples of their work and got more than thirty serious responses. In November 2003, Adam Bregenzer and I launched grouphug.us version 2. It looked the same but I was able to add an unlimited number of moderators to help read through confessions and vote to decide the fate of each submission.

November also brought the first big bit of press. I'd had some write-ups in smaller publications (Venus,[7] Defunktion,[8] a few others) but the *New York Post* two-page

6. gabrieljeffrey.com/log.

7. venuszine.com.

8. defunktion.net.

spread on November 23 was *the shit.* Never mind the bad clip art, the cover of that issue was Michael Jackson's disemnosed facehead. It doesn't get any more legitimate.

In February 2004 I went to Austin, Texas, to work on another project. On a walk to get coffee one morning through a South Austin neighborhood, my mobile phone rang and showed a blocked number.

"Hello?"

"Mr. Jeffrey?"

"Yes."

"Is this Mr. Gabriel Jeffrey?"

"Yes, this is Mr. Gabriel Jeffrey."

"Do you own grouphug.us?"

"Yup."

"This is the Secret Service."

"Okay."

"We're concerned about a note on your Web site. We would like to contact the individual who wrote this note. Can you help us contact the individual who wrote this note?"

"No."

"There's no way to contact the individual?"

"No, the site is anonymous. There's no way to contact them."

"Anonymous? Can you please explain how it's anonymous?"

"Well, the server keeps no visitor logs. Um, all we record is the date, the text they type, and a random number."

"A random number?"

"A random number."

"Okay. Thank you."

"Wait. What did the confession say?"

"It threatened the life of the President of the United States."

"Oh, okay. Bye."

That's the story I tell when someone asks me how I guarantee anonymity. If the United States Secret Service is satisfied, well, some of those guys are pretty smart. They all look like they must have MBAs or something. And their phone voices are *hot*.

I started compiling this book in the spring of 2004, when there were already over 50,000 confessions approved by the screeners and visible on grouphug.us. After months of reading confessions, they really all start to look the same. It made it impossible to find the "best" confessions, which of course is relative to begin with. My approach became to find the most representative confessions, to distill tens of thousands of pages of personal confessions into a palmable document. This was made insanely difficult by the massive amount of content. I could easily do a volume of the funniest, one of the nastiest, another of those that I wish were mine, and a series of tomes with the worst spelling you've seen in your life.

There are no points for spelling and grammar online, which means that I had a hard choice to make in the editing of this book. One of my favorite examples of a typical submission:

160342055

i found out somthing that feels real good but i thinks its bad. in the bathtub i put my croch under the fawcet and its great but i always feel gilty after. like i did somthing bad. also my mom is getting suspishus cause i take so many baths a day and i ddidnt used to.

There are some that are completely incomprehensible, and there are gems like this one where the awful spelling is part of the message. This is a public record of a middle school kid discovering her crotch. Half of this story is lost with any editing.

Ultimately, I decided to lightly edit the confessions for spelling and punctuation. There are instances where I felt that a misspelling or bit of vernacular was worth

preserving, so here's a damn handy guide to *l'Internet
moderne vernaculaire:*

Vernacular	Meaning
:)	happy face
:(	sad face
wtf?	what the fuck?
gf	girlfriend
bf	boyfriend
coz, cuz	because
omg	oh my god
35/m	35-year-old male
17/f	35-year-old ugly, fat, bald male *or* 17-year-old female
meh	onomatopoeia indicating cool indifference
im	instant message
live journal	livejournal.com: a popular place to emote and be messily emoted upon
a/s/l	age/sex/location
wanna cyber?	would you care to have "cyber sex?"
wtfomgbbq	what the fuck oh my god barbeque

For confession purists, you'll notice that each confession has a number — completely random — with which you can reference the original, unmolested confession at grouphug.us/book.

By the way, I've decided to make a few personal confessions throughout this book: smelling my own farts, so to speak. Enjoy.

shame

For a short time in my 4s I went to a day care in a large house in Omaha, Nebraska. It was just getting dark when the woman with black hair announced that we were to collect our mats for napping. Mine that day was a shiny blue workout mat with fancy musculature printed on it in white. I was wearing a red fire helmet. I was dozing, thinking about the day behind me and all that I'd accomplished (throwing sand, finding an abandoned juice box and drinking it, sucking scandalously before the owner returned) when I crapped my pants. Hot and not firm enough to run with, I sort of kneeled uncomfortably for the rest of naptime. What seemed something like nineteen hours later — as kids started milling around looking for parents — I edged to the bathroom, sort of scraped out what I could, and then sidled out to find my mom. This little fire fighter rode home with the window down that night.

674479928

When I was a young kid (but probably old enough to know better), for some unfathomable reason I took a shit on the carpet in the living room. I then told my mom the cat had done it. I'm still horrified to think that I actually did that.

275303023

One time I was backstage at a Dave Matthews show (who

I can't stand) and I got so bored I went to the bathroom to masturbate. I thought I locked the door but I didn't and the drummer, Carter, walked in on me.

360021994

One time while working at a restaurant, a woman and her daughter came in. Her daughter was wearing a big coat with a hood and I couldn't see her face. I grabbed a regular menu and a kid's menu and sat them down. Then the daughter took off her coat and it was a full-grown midget! She asked for a regular menu and I ran and got one, avoiding eye contact the rest of their meal.

190262613

I had been a virgin until my late late teens, and my general lack of any sex drive didn't help the matter. A good friend of mine had recently become overly fed up with my supposed "weakness" one night while we were drinking at [his] house, so he proceeded to grab my cell phone when I wasn't paying attention, and called every female name I had in my phone book in alphabetical order (which I later found out included my best friend, neighbor, and my mother).

He managed to successfully invite over a friend of mine (at the time) who was already mildly intoxicated. His full-blown intentions were to get me laid, and he made this painfully obvious from the moment she set foot in the house. After an hour or so of flirting, massages, and eventual second base activity, he suggested that her and I move our fun to the spare bedroom across the hall. One thing led to another, and we ended up having sex.

Keeping in mind the common myth that male virgins tend to ejaculate rather quickly, I tried everything I could to keep my mind off of the pleasure I was experiencing.

This ended up being a big mistake, as we found ourselves making drunken love for hours on end. Before we knew it, the scent of coffee was filling the room, and I noticed there was a lot more light filling into the room through the window.

We both simultaneously figured that my instigating friend's father was waking up to go to work, and instantly jumped into a clothes-finding panic. Both of us were dressed and calm within roughly 30 seconds, and while I was putting on my shoes, his father slowly opens the door. We look up at him as sober and docile as we possibly could, and after staring at us for a moment, he says,

"I don't know what you two were doing in here, but you need to get the hell out of this room."

As it turns out, I had just lost my virginity on the same bed that my (instigating) friend's grandmother spent her last month alive on. She passed away in her sleep less than 24 hours prior to the occasion.

490186838

People think that I'm very sophisticated and chic — men often compliment me by telling me I'm beautiful and classy. Here's a little secret: I pick my nose and eat the boogers, I **never** wipe, I peed in my very expensive, silk pants yesterday, so I just splashed some talc powder on the crotch and am wearing them again today. My room is a mess. I stuff my bra. I apply concealer very well in order to hide the massive amounts of acne and scars on my cheeks (ironically enough, everyone always compliments me on my "perfect" skin). I wear the same socks (and go running in them) for sometimes a week in a row. I have unruly, hairy pubic hair, which I only shave if I know that I'm going to get some action. I also have rather hairy nipples, which I also shave if an "occasion" is coming up. Oh yeah, did I mention that I pee in the steam room and public showers in my gym?

815065711

I kind of miss high school. Isn't that pathetic?

667542951

I was waiting for my family to pick me up at my apartment for a big family dinner, but they were coming late. So I sat in front of the TV and started to channel surf. I was quickly distracted by a "Wild On" episode with Brooke Burke wearing nothing but a bikini in the Bahamas. After a few intense moments at staring at her perfect bare belly, I decided to whip out the old hand cream and pulled down my pants and began masturbating. It was pretty intense. I turned up the intensity trying to make sure that I came before the next commercial break. Then suddenly I heard the door jar wide open, and my entire family walked in my living room, with my hand stuck on my peter. There was an initial shock of surprise, but I knew I couldn't stop, so I jizzed in front of my family. I ran back into the bathroom in front of their petrified faces, where I washed my hands and grabbed some toilet paper to clean up after myself.

350419817

For years I never knew what POW-MIA meant so I sort of mocked it, now I know and feel like a shit head.

728014205

One day while riding the elevator up to my office, I farted. It felt really hot, and when I sat down in my chair, I noticed a damp feeling in my pants. I walked to the restroom to check, and I had pooped in my pants. I threw my underwear away and cleaned up the best that I could. But because I had ridden the bus to work, I had to wait at the bus stop with other people and a stain on the seat of my pants. I untucked my shirt, but it didn't cover it.

When the bus finally came, I sat next to a bum so that if I stunk, the other people would hopefully think it was the bum who smelled like crap.

892735194

When I was 13 my grandfather caught me rubbing one out and asked if he could help. I said no thanks I've got it under control. He shrugged and walked away.

393845560

I want to be somebody else.

403401007

One time I wanted a chicken parm sub so badly that I cried.

174460748

When I was 12, I had a cockatiel named Charlie. I liked to hold Charlie. I also liked to sleep. The two didn't mix well together. I fell asleep holding poor Charlie and rolled over on him. He didn't survive.

293729543

I'm a woman and I work in a man's world as an electrician. I try to be badass like all the other guys, but I am so lonely in this shit town.

976909609

When I was in grade school I was always perfectly behaved. When the students would get in trouble we would have to "move our pen" on the bulletin board, and after that happened like 10 times they would call our parents.
Needless to say, I had never had to "move my pen" almost up until the end of the year. But one time, I forgot my homework at home, which would make me have to...but the teacher didn't make me.

I reminded her that all the other students had to when they forgot their homework in the past, so she told me to "move my pen", and I did, and I flipped out. I start crying and getting all emotional, and the teacher made me go sit outside in the hall.

Ironically after this one offense, the teacher called my parents cause I took it so poorly.

895072294

I've only cried at two movies...
It's a Wonderful Life, as one should and *Home Alone* ...Why this movie, when so many more deserve it...kills me inside.

360212961

I hate living, I've been in a wheelchair just over a year and a half now... I feel like a ghost watching the people around me enjoy being alive, while I can't experience an ounce of the fun.

I even have the cutest and sexiest girlfriend in the world (and I don't mean this in a complementary or romanticizing way, personality aside even, she is F'ing hot), but

I can't fully enjoy being with her physically (because I can't feel from the waist down) and she pretends that it doesn't bother her, but I see the disappointment in her eyes every time she hungrily goes down on me or rides me only to find that I can't even get a hard-on.

It makes me laugh and seethe with rage too, when everyone sees old people loosing control of their bodies or people getting crippled on TV, and say that they're better off dead. But when they talk to me, they say how fortunate I am, not to have died in the shooting that paralyzed me.

If I were normal, I would have everything in my life right now: girl, free college, wealth, and fun. But since I'm only half a man, I go thru this meaningless life devoid of anything beyond minute, short-lived, happiness. It's really fucking pathetic to be half dead/half alive, so I'll end it soon. Just so you know though, love, religion, and hope are illusions that exist only to make people feel better about screwing, heartache, and change and if you don't believe it, become paralyzed, observe, and be honest (with self and others).

655318270

I'm absolutely convinced I'm **fat and ugly and horrible**. People tell me I'm not and I'm the opposite. My boyfriend says I'm the most beautiful girl he's ever seen but I'm sure he's just saying it. I came out 3rd best looking in my year in a poll at my school but I'm sure they just feel sorry for me.

I look at other people and I'm so jealous. I am a size 10/12, I am a 34D breast size, aged 16, I'm 5'8", I have long brown hair and hazel eyes. It's just every time I look in the mirror I see **fat** and I'm so ashamed of my body I keep my coat on at all time even when I'm at school in lessons. If I say 2 my mum, "Do I look fat?" she says, "Well your not skinny...." My bf said its just because she's jealous she's just lost a lot of weight and she wishes her boobs were as big as mine.

Every time I eat I feel guilty but I just can't stop myself. Sometimes I can go a week without eating but it doesn't stay and I know it's unhealthy but diets don't work!!!

I cut myself. I hate myself so much I can't bear 2 look in the mirror. I wish I was **dead**. I contemplate that every day but I never get round 2 it...plus my mum said if I ever did that then I'd b a coward and she'd hate me forever for it.

But how can I b worth anything? My dad has just said he doesn't want anymore to do with me, he doesn't need me any more he's got another girlfriend with 5 **children** and he wants them. Half of my family **hate me** and don't talk to me any more because they hate my dad because he's an arse and I wanted him at my last birthday party (b4 he abandoned me) there was a massive argument and now **none** of them want me.

Am I really that bad?

819301837

I don't know what to do anymore. The one person in the world I truly loved the most, my fiancée, has left me. I've never felt this much pain before in my life. I don't think any amount of physical pain could compare. I've lost it all, and feel that if things don't change, I'll wind up taking my own life soon. The thought of suicide has been on my mind a lot lately. I don't want to hurt those that know me by doing this, especially my son, but I don't think I can go on this way. The worst feeling in the world, is loving someone deeply and knowing they no longer love you back. I'm torn apart inside. I want to die.

557109704

I am fat and ugly and no one could ever possibly find me at all attractive. I always bemoan the fact that everyone is so shallow, but even I find myself disgusting. Plus, I don't have a good personality either. I am a total loser. I am stupid, annoying, mean, and pathetic. Even if I weren't ugly, there is no reason that anyone would ever like me, but I still blame other people for being shallow.

424618389

Whenever my parents leave the house, I just have to say goodbye to them. I feel that if I don't, something bad will happen to them. I am terrified of knowing that someday, a goodbye will be the last thing I ever say to them, but it's better than saying nothing. I love them so much and I worry about them all the time.

303167254

I miss my brother so much. He was shot and killed earlier this year. I really miss him and I spent most of the night crying about it. I didn't get to really know him like I wanted to. I miss him so much.

742790773

My Weenie Is Tiny. *cries*

531804531

When I was 7yo this girl had a crush on me. She said one day that she'd like to show me her bits after school. I told her that this was a great idea and I'd meet her in the BMX park afterwards — and then I told everybody in the whole school that she was going to get naked after school.

Needless to say about 100 boys showed up in the BMX park and she was on top of a little gravel hill surrounded by them. They were all shouting at her to display, and she was beetroot red. Amazingly, she gave in under so much incredible pressure and took off her skirt and panties, then eventually started crying.

Next day she got called to the headmaster's office along with a bunch of other people in a general school inquiry. For some reason I was never asked about it by anybody in authority.

She got moved to another school. I thought about this because I saw her the other day and she gave me a really nasty look :(

832236780

My girlfriend and I take turns reading out loud to each other. The other night, when we finished the last book we were reading, I was in tears.

What a fucking pussy.

327661281

One time when I was in second grade we had to make kites. We all got to fly them outside and everyone was having lots of fun. I was running around with my mouth gaping open from laughing until suddenly I smacked into this other kid's face and inadvertently bit his eyeball out. There was blood everywhere and all the kids started crying. And so ended kite day.

50051327

The worst thing I've ever done — the thing that plagues
me at night — is that when my mom was sick and dying
of cancer, I was sitting there on the couch opposite the
chair she was in just reading a Star Trek novel (*Spock's
World* for those Trek absorbed few out there) and it was
engrossing. My mom was sitting there feeling like shit
and I was reading and she said to me "So are you
keeping me company?" and I was too fucking engrossed
in the book to put it down and talk to her for a bit. I was
actually irritated at the interruption. Her last fucking
cogent day on earth and I read a stupid fucking Trek
novel instead of holding her and talking to her. I just said
"Yeah I guess so..." and went back to my fucking book.
She died the next day. I would give anything I possess to
be able to chat with her for a moment now. Anything.

496289646

I pretend I'm perfect but in fact I hate myself for being
such a jerk.

758464160

I think my parents are stupid. I'm embarrassed that I'm
their son, because that means I'm probably stupid too. I
told my mother that.

526939102

I really hurt my girlfriend's feelings and now I'm not sure
if we're gonna go out anymore. We both know that we're
in love with each other but she's really hurt and I can't
stand it coz what I said I didn't mean. Normally I'm the
one that she turns to if she has a problem but because it
was me who hurt her she can't. I'm worried that she'll go
back to her ex.

She knows how sorry I am but I don't know if she'll be able to trust me anymore and that was really the basis of our relationship, we told each other everything. I really hate myself for making her feel this way, and because she feels bad, I feel crap. I can't take it anymore!

528626929

I hate people who press the button at a crossing when the wait sign is already lit, I feel as though they are questioning my button pressing abilities. My friend did this earlier today and I hit him really hard. I don't think he deserved that.

734643859

Yesterday, I was one day shy of the end of my diet... but suddenly I decided to binge. Today, too. And I gained back like 4 pounds. ARGH. I'm so fucking pissed with myself.

630822148

I just want to get it all out... I'm 14...I lost my virginity when I was 12. I smoke pot too much and drink too much. I think I'm going to die...I want to have sex with my boyfriend (15) and we've only been going out for 2 days. I've tried to kill myself...and still often think of suicide. Is there something wrong with me?

716515906

There's a girl I really like. I'm totally obsessed with her.

Problem is, she has a boyfriend, for two years now.

We're very good friends and I don't want to ruin our relationship by telling her what I feel. I do want her to break up with her boyfriend, whom I think doesn't treat her good at all.

This weekend we went to a party without her bf, and she brought another friend of hers with us.

In the morning me and my friends went home, while she and her friend stayed. He told her he loves her, too.

Now I'm not sure whether I should have told her or not. I really love her and I've never even had a chance.

Life does suck sometimes.

352690506

I live the kind of life that lots of others envy, but I think of suicide every day. Life is little more than a way to find love, and that seems impossible to me now.

190199034

I hate crabs, they scare the shit out of me. The animal, not the STD. I'd much rather have crabs than actually deal with the crustacean crab.

371854250

My boyfriend just broke up with me, and now I'm hoping I get some horrible illness or suffer some huge tragedy so he'll pity me.

609895370

Ew, he's so gross and ugly. I can't believe I did that with him. :(

117529089

I "experimented" in college. I hooked up with this one guy online, walked over to his dorm, and we made out and groped each other. Then I sucked his cock. When I finished, he went to suck me and had a seizure. I haven't fooled around with anyone (men or women) since that. I heard he was okay later on, but he never called me back or anything.

Sometimes I wonder if he could have faked the seizure.

925319853

I just found out that somebody I used to fool around with has herpes, and I think I have it!

38072311

Sometimes I want to leave it all behind me...my husband, kids, friends. Just leave, and start a whole new life. I lay in bed at night and think about what I would do, where I would go. I guess I miss the freedom...or perhaps the desire to be selfish.

880625227

If I run out of shortbread cookies, I get inexplicably pissed off. One time I peed in my roommate's shoes because he forgot to buy my cookies at the store.

215931900

Once when I was a small child, I was playing hide and go seek at a birthday party, hid underneath a bed, and waited for my cousin to come out of his hiding place. After he did, I then grabbed a metal baton and cracked him in the back until he fell down.

817365743

I threw rocks at a homeless guy once. I was young and wrong. If you are an ex-homeless guy, who once had rocks thrown at him, and who now is successful enough to get on the Internet, I'm sorry guy.

960924465

My cat was hit by a car. In my own garage.

135659054

I'm gay and at the age of 18 I learned about the world of tea rooms. A tea room for those of you that don't know is a public bathroom in which men meet to have sex at. This all started one day when I went to the bathroom at my college after one of my classes ended. I noticed there was a hole in the wall and I peeked through it. What I saw was a handsome guy jacking off and putting on a show. I stared in amazement and watched him jack off. I finally got nervous when someone else came in the restroom and I left immediately. I kept thinking about it days afterwards and jacking off thinking about it. I went back the next school week and learned about gloryholes and started reading the writing on the walls. I started blowing guys before classes and after classes and getting blowjobs.

I was doing it because I was depressed and felt bitter at the fact that I hadn't met a potential boyfriend. This happened at school a lot and I ended up skipping a lot of classes. This lead to even more random anonymous encounters at bathhouses and meeting guys off the Internet for sex. I'm glad that I haven't gotten AIDS or anything and I've since calmed down in the past year. I'm still depressed and horribly lonely. I hope my soul mate (if I do have one) forgives me for my past sexual actions.

I only gave these men my bodies but not my heart.

482473720

I've lived in New York for most of my adult life. I left Tinytown after college to live here, and have never seriously considered going back or going anywhere else.

On September 11, 2001, nobody from my family contacted me. The buildings were coming down right outside my office window, it was scary as hell, and I called home to tell everyone I was still alive. No one called back for days, and in the months since then any time we talk about that they elevate the discussion up to where they have always elevated conversations that have anything to do with New York City: they talk as if I am not really here, as if I see the things that happen here the way they see them: as packaged television events. As if what happened here on 9/11 happened only on newsreel and was not a real event. They still talk like I'm not really here but except that I'm trying to prove something.

Now when something happens to me, whether it's good, bad or who knows what, I stop and think about whether or not I should bother anyone at home with the news. Since September 11th I mostly don't bother, and I try to handle it the way they do: I'll tell them about my life if our paths cross, if they happen to call on the phone for some unrelated reason, or I'll tell them what's new with me the next time I happen to hit the road to Tinytown and they happen to still be there. But I'm not going out of my way. It seems wrong, because I used to call and tell all whenever there was anything to tell. But I guess things change in life. Or maybe they don't.

489438697

After 9/11, I was disappointed that the whole thing didn't turn into an all out nuclear world war...I'm simply ready to stop working and start searching for food and water...I'd rather go bald and bleed out of my ass than spend one more minute in this cube...is this what God had in mind?

965302768

I was gang raped when I was 14 and as a result I had to abort an unborn innocent child. My family know nothing and only a few friends do. I've tried counseling but I can't speak to someone who doesn't know me — I don't want them to make any judgments which they will. Each day gets harder and I can't cope with a real relationship. I'm now 21 and need some kind of outlet but all I can do is cry for a child unborn. A life I took away so selfishly and even, I guess with malice. I'd like to say the boys got what they wanted but they didn't take anything away from me but it's not true. I'm a shell of a human. Everyone I meet tells me how special I am and how wonderful I am and how it's so good to have someone like me in their life but they don't know I'm a ruthless murderer. Deep down I think I know I was right to terminate the pregnancy — how could I have given this child all it needed? All the love every child deserves? Knowing that they weren't conceived with love? How do I get through this without losing my mind?

524086943

I was addressing Christmas cards at work the other day using my best cursive handwriting, and it looked really, really good to me, and I started thinking of all of these weird things, like people receiving the cards looking at the handwriting and thinking it was the most beautiful thing they'd ever seen, and then coming and searching for me and then I became famous for my handwriting. I felt really, really stupid for thinking it, but it was nice at the same time. I'm too embarrassed about it to tell my friends, so I'm glad I found this site.

429254819

Once when I was driving home on the toll road, I considered driving into the barricade and killing myself just because I wondered how many people/who from school would show up at my funeral and be emotionally devastated at my death.

It actually made me feel better about myself.

406352894

I used to love a girl. And she loved me. We did a lot of drugs together, never left each other's side, and meant the world to each other. Then I got her pregnant, and she had an abortion while I was away.

We stopped talking over the summer. Then I sobered up. When I came back to school, all of a sudden I became popular and well liked. People started to recognize me and I became respected. The public eye...I have no secrets from anyone anymore, and every step I take seems to register a ripple effect where I live. Every time I see her, my heart tells me that I never stopped loving her. And everyone can see that...

She wants me, and I want to tell her that I do too. I want to fuck away the hurt that we caused each other. I want to show people how much we love each other, and I want to stop caring about what everyone thinks all the time.

I know that I shouldn't be putting people's opinion of me first, especially when the person that I love most is a phone call away.

I am scared [of] taking her back, because I don't want to become the old me.

I can't stop thinking about her. I miss holding her tight.

I wish I was braver.

819011722

My closest friend and I applied to the same extremely prestigious college for early action. I know that he had better credentials than I did and expected him to get in.

When the day the decisions came out, I was rejected and I called my friend. When he was opening his letter, I was secretly hoping he would not get in so that he could be miserable like me. Fortunately, he didn't get in either and I was absolutely relieved. Is that selfish?

683769501

I'm 12 years old. Last week I found out I was pregnant from having sex with this kid at my school. I don't know what to tell my parents or how to. I just started my period like a month ago.

479046270

I started the Ash Wednesday of Melbourne Australia in 1983. My friends and I were 15/16 at the time. We were playing with firecrackers and petrol. We lit one a bit too big. Fortunately the fire incinerated the evidence and no one ever found out. We swore to secrecy and we never told anyone. My friend moved away and I haven't spoken to him since.

Looking back I feel a little bit bad.

455248847

I'm completely fake. At school I pretend I'm all laid back and don't care what I'm wearing, but in reality I'm totally self conscience and comb my hair in order to make is look uncombed. I hate nearly everyone I pretend to like and have more than once come within an inch of stealing my parent's car and taken off, to get away from these people.

933645720

I try to watch movies that make me cry. Most of the time I don't. I just want to feel human.

249135566

I made plans to travel across the country and meet a man I am truly crazy about, but something horrible happened that prevented me from going. I have just spent the last 4 hours trying to decide what I'm more upset about. The horrible thing, or missing out on spending a weekend with this incredible man.

Oh, I also put barbeque sauce on just about everything I eat.

226710467

My life sucks. I get up, go to school, come home, do homework for hours on end, and then I go to sleep in preparation to do it the next day. The monotony is absolutely excruciating, so I try to trick myself into thinking I'm a secure and happy person by acting funny and unique around my friends, when in fact I'm bored and depressed. To try and remedy my boredom by playing a lot of games and masturbating at least twice a day sometimes to gay porn, which I struggle to keep hidden and deleted because I am secretly bi-curious (taboo subject in my culture). I wish just once I could have sex with a boy but I'm afraid to advance because I might get shot down and labeled the bull queer at my small school. Don't get me wrong I like girls too but something about a muscular, smooth school buddy pounding my ass excites me.

185793286

I am jealous of everyone around me.

It's not that they are smarter, hotter, more talented, more charismatic, more likeable, etc. etc. etc. I'm not jealous of people who are flat out better than me — they deserve better.

I'm jealous of the people who are on my level. I am jealous of the people who have everything fall into their lap, while I bust my ass with nothing to show for it.

I'm jealous of my roommate for getting a job offer from the one company I even care about. His GPA is about .02 higher than mine. Our work/research experience is about equal. But he didn't even have to apply. **They** came to **him** saying they need someone to fill so and so position, and would he be interested. Meanwhile, I speak to their reps every term, modify my class schedule to suit their liking, talk with them in depth about the company, and I don't even get a bloody interview.

I'm jealous of my friends with lower GPAs, little relevant experience, and nothing special to make them stand out who spend 5 minutes submitting their resume and have an interview the next day. I haven't gotten a single interview this year, even from the companies that guaranteed I would get one.

I'm jealous of people who are in committed relationships. I'm jealous of everyone who can say someone cares about him more than anyone else. I'm jealous of everyone who has someone to hold and someone to be held by. I'm jealous of everyone who has a warm body to sleep next to.

I'm jealous of every man I see who's shorter, fatter, uglier, dorkier, more awkward, or in any other way worse off than me but has the kind of girlfriend I would kill for. I'm jealous of everyone who says and does all the wrong things and still gets the girl. I don't even get the girl when I say and do the right things. I've been so desperate at times I bought books on how to succeed. And yet I'm still here, jealous of everyone else.

I'm jealous of the ugly Asian guy with the beautiful dance partner. I'm jealous of the lanky, weird-looking kid I know from high school with the personality of wood who has the kind of girl I'd donate my kidneys for. I'm jealous of the guys my gorgeous project group-mate calls in the wee hours of the night when she's drunk. I've never been one of those guys. I'm jealous of every guy who's fucked her.

I'm jealous of everyone who's happy with how he looks. I'm jealous of everyone who eats hamburgers and ice cream and works out once a month and still looks better than me. I watch what I eat and work out 6 times a week, and I still can't take those last 3–4 inches off my belt.

I'm jealous of everyone with a huge family and relatives all across the country. I'm jealous of everyone who has family get-togethers during the holidays. The only family I have are my parents.

I'm jealous of everyone who has direction in his life. I'm

jealous of everyone who has plans for the future. I'm jealous of everyone who knows where he'll be in a year. I'm jealous of everyone who knows what he's doing with his life.

I'm jealous of everyone who never had to learn things the hard way. I'm jealous of everyone who didn't have to learn from mistakes. I'm jealous of everyone who's always had things work themselves out.

I'm so full of hatred it makes me sick. I'm tired of putting up an act for everyone else. I'm tired of giving advice like I know what I'm doing and twisting stories so they make me look better. I never have to lie, but I always have to bend the truth. No one would ever guess that I'm so alone, so unsuccessful, so useless, so desperate. I could never tell them.

I'm bitter and resentful. I put in the time and effort and I have nothing to show for it. There are so many things I would pray for if I could make myself believe in prayer.

If you're the praying kind, I beg you to add in a prayer for me next time. I don't want to be this way anymore.

534470047

It's been a little over a year now that I literally haven't left the house. I'm gonna be 25 years old soon and I live with my mom. She tells me to get a job but all I do is sitting in front of the computer all day and learn about graphic design. I haven't been talking to any of my few friends in that period of time. I'm like stuck in here and nobody can help me. I'm not even sure if somebody could. Even though I could have contact with a lot of people over the Internet, I don't feel like chatting with anybody. I'm a hardcore loner with a lazy attitude.

521167251

I am annoyed with my children tonight. I am annoyed that I don't have a thousand dollars to spend on Christmas this year, and instead, only three hundred. I am mad that I wrecked my hot rod, and now I am driving a piece of shit Ford Taurus rental car. I am sexually frustrated and I wish my husband would initiate sex sometimes so I don't have to beg for it. My feet hurt from new shoes. I wish I had big boobs. Okay that's enough. I'm feeling better already.

740485209

I tried to cut myself so I would feel better. It only made the pain worse. Then I got more depressed because I thought I couldn't even do that right!

90511518

When I was in middle school I started smoking to be cool. I couldn't let my parents know, so I did it in my room next to the window. One night I left a lit cigarette on the windowsill while I went to answer the phone and a house fire started that resulted in my youngest sister dying of smoke inhalation. My dad blamed my mom, who always smokes in the house and they got a divorce. I never told them the truth.

228420043

I don't have any close friends that are blokes. I still wish I was with my ex. I have crushes on the two closes friends I have. I've never given a girl an orgasm. I fall in love with people I meet briefly and end up just speaking to them online. I can't find anyone that I click with who lives any suitable distance from me. I like being emo. I pretend I'm an individual when all I do is copy people that the people I don't know see, thus "ooo look, isn't he individual."

943500966

I'm extremely self-conscious about my neck. I'm a girl and I have an adam's apple. You think I would give a shit about boobs or a big butt or misplaced fat tissue or whatever girls worry about, but it's just my neck. I hate it. My voice is sort of ugly and low. It sounds horrible. I'm saving up right now to have surgery done. I want the two bulges (I don't know what the other one is) to just go away so I can throw my head back and laugh without another shitty remark about my neck.

479228577

There's this one girl I asked to homecoming. I made my own fortune cookies and put a word in each, and strung them together. It spelled "Will you go to Homecoming with me?" But after lunch, I remembered that she was severely allergic to galvanized sugar, which was what I used to make them. Obviously she had some, cuz I found out later that she got her stomach pumped, but it was too late. Her liver couldn't process it, and now she needs a new liver. I would give her mine, but I don't think it's worth it. Then I can't go to Homecoming. Plus, we're probably not the same blood type so yea. Sorry though.

666069155

I suspect I was molested as a child. I don't know why I think this.

902403325

I voted for John Howard in 1994, what the fuck have we done.

830110037

I really am a nice girl, with morals somewhere inside me, and self-respect, but I slept with 5 people in the first 2 months of college (including 3 in one weekend! Thursday-Friday-Saturday). I was only dating one of these guys, but that ended in a week and a half.

What kind of slut sleeps with 3 people in one weekend? I hear my friends say all the time, "Oh my god, I heard about this girl on our floor who slept with 4 people since she got here!" And I shake my head and say, "Shame on her." When really I'm thinking — wow. Guess I'm a whore in the eyes of the world.

But really, I don't have any intention of changing my behavior. I'm fine. But I'd be so embarrassed if anyone knew, I haven't even told my best-best friend...everyone would lose respect for me.

9120932

I tried to kill myself when I was 13.

367299852

I told my friend not to invite his other friend to our camping trip one time because I was jealous of the attention I would miss out on, and that night the guy we didn't invite died in a car wreck on his way home from another friend's house. And I feel somewhat responsible for his death.

235172338

I have just recently dropped my guitar pick in the toilet and I have this very bad habit of putting it into my mouth whenever I have to stop and read the music and I don't think I can stop.

The 2-liter hydrogen bomb experiment was a sham for which I was awarded an unmerited A+. In defense of the good mark: as a teacher of the Science Arts, Mr. Hostetler really ought to have known better. My plan to ace the science fair was to produce a small amount of hydrogen gas, fill a 2-liter soda bottle with it, and blow up the whole works out on the soccer field. Visions of a great crater. Honestly, I'm not sure if I even managed to produce the gas, as every attempt to electronically ignite the thing failed miserably. Initial trials used standard phone equipment and a little igniter thingy from a model rocket set. The side effect of this was that it could be wired to a house phone, which would cause it to spark when the handset was lifted, and was widely regarded as a bad idea. The design a miserable failure, I hid some solid explosives from the rocket set in the plastic cap of the bottle before the public demonstration. Students and teachers alike were amazed and terrified by the awesome pop and wisp of smoke that gray afternoon.

565792187

My boyfriend cheated on me so I shaved off my pubes and baked them in a cake. Then watched when he scoffed the lot.

325830553

I am madly in love with my boyfriend of many years,

who I will marry one day. But I kind of rolled around with some guy a few years ago and never told anyone, not even my best friend. The "other" guy had a thing for me, and it was exciting being wanted by someone else.

So, I called him to wish him a happy birthday and he never called me back. Then I found out that this guy was so torn up about not being able to be with me that he blocked me!

Cock Sucker.

307218929

I love my girlfriend with all my heart. But given a chance and some liquid courage, there's a girl in Canada I'm dying to get with, and also a girl downstate I would kill to screw. Send me to hell now, please, would you?

745864926

It wasn't supposed to end up this way, but it did. I once loved someone so much. He was my best friend and was the best lover I have ever had. I had small children when we met and he wasn't ready for that. After three years of waiting for him to be ready, I decided he was not ever going to be ready to take on my kids. I felt that our relationship would never develop because of this and I felt that I was choosing him over my kids. Even though I loved him very much, I broke off our relationship. I ended up dating and eventually marring another man. I married him because I accidentally got pregnant. And yes, I loved him. He turned out to be abusive, physically, and mentally.

My ex moved his new girlfriend in, who had a kid. Something he was totally opposed to when we were dating. That hurt my feelings a little, but I was married so I guess it really wasn't my business. We had been friends since high school with a small group of people and a couple times a year we all get together. This did not change. Every time I saw him, I knew I still loved him. But it didn't hurt to see him. I was always happy to.

About two years into my fucked up marriage, all of us got together for one of our reunions. He was there and I hadn't seen him in like a year. We all ended up at his place to spend the night as we had all drank too much. My best friend (a girl) and I were out in the living room falling asleep on the couches and he was in his room. I felt compelled to go into his room. It wasn't purely sexual, I just wanted to lay in his arms again.

He seemed to be thinking the same thing cause when I walked into his room, he just opened his blanket and I laid down. We spooned and made some jokes about how I was married and how wrong this was. Then I broke down and bawled and told him all the bad things that were going on in my marriage and he held me and let me cry. Then he told me that he had never stopped loving me. That for two years he had tried and that he couldn't stop. He had stopped seeing his girlfriend, but missed her son. He told me he was ready for kids, and that's when the affair started.

Consequently, my husband found out. I told my ex that I had to stop. That I felt shitty about what I had done and that made what we had shitty. He totally understood this, we stayed in contact but we weren't sleeping together.

He told me he was going to move away. Far away. I was very sad. I wanted to be with him. He told me to leave my husband and go with him. I almost did. But I couldn't stop thinking. He is single, no kids. I would be an albatross around his neck. So I let him go. I said that I was going to leave my husband, and I did. But I told him I wasn't ready to get into another relationship. LIE.

All I wanted was for him to be happy. And I felt that I would complicate his life. He left thinking I didn't love him anymore. He still lives far away from me. We still talk and email once or twice a month. He has another girlfriend, and he sounds happy. So why when I talk to him does he sound like he wants to tell me he loves me but can't?? I feel like I made his choice for him and we both have to live with it. I thought I was doing the right thing, but now I wonder. I have another boyfriend too. He is great. He takes care of me like a queen, loves my children and I wish I loved him as much as I love my ex. I hope I will be with him later on in life. Even if we are both 60.

564980242

So I'm on a wireless network link, and for some reason it was sucking.

So, being the dork I am, I fired up a packet-capture. It ran for a few minutes, and picked up nothing at all abnormal.

And then I noticed that Ethereal could sort by protocol type.

And that AIM was one of the protocols.

And that my mom was apparently sending someone messages. And that I could read them.

So I read them. And instantly regretted it.

Turns out she's having an affair with some bloke from

work. It's been months, now, and the signs keep growing. I feel so dirty for helping her configure her iPaq to use our wireless network and some mysterious third party's mail servers... I know exactly whose mail servers those are and I know exactly what sort of e-mail she's sending. I picked up her iPaq one day and she *totally flipped out.* Heh.

I'm also guilty of reading over her shoulder sometimes. When we're in the SUV on a trip down to the beach and she's sitting there with her laptop and a cellular modem card... ugh.

I wonder if my dad knows.

... But god only knows he's been staying up to strange hours on his laptop, recently.

I shouldn't be so suspicious.

Makes you wonder about people, though, really...

970112446

I just swore on my kid that I'm not sleeping with my friend — but I am, and I might even leave my husband to be with him. But probably not. I really hope the baby wakes up in the morning.

316455666

I am a junior high band director and I hate my job. I used to be the director and music chairman for the district, but due to an exposed encounter a few years back, I lost my job. I engaged in an affair with an advisor for the band and shared a room on the spring trip. Unfortunately, one of the other advisors attempted to enter our room at night because of a student incident. This was the worst event of my life, next to losing a finger.

275281115

I'm in the 7th grade and about 2 weeks ago, I was standing with my girlfriend and her friends. This one chick has her tongue pierced 3 times and was licking this ice cream thing. God this girl has the most gorgeous mouth I have ever seen, like really white skin, perfect shaped, perfect colored lips with really pale lip gloss.... so anyway, she was like eating this ice cream thing and GOD it got me soo turned on that I rushed to the bathroom and masturbated. Since that day I have had an obsession with mouths. I stole the girl's chapstick a few times just so I can watch her lick her lips in class... I would kill my girlfriend just to have this girl give me oral sex. I really would...

859487343

Last night, I went over a grrrlbuddy's apartment to hang out and 420 like usual. I've liked her for a while and I'm sure she knows. We've gotten together after a drunken stupor before. But she's really into girls and have hot girlfriends coming over all the time.

This time, her two best girlfriends just started making out hardcore on the couch. They started taking their pants off and just got buck wild! I was all into it and my grrrlbuddy was all "jump in, dude." So...I did. I don't know how it ended up but next thing you know it was just me and her bestest friend just fully going mouth porn. But, my grrrlbuddy, who I really like, didn't join. I was bummed. Today, I find out that her girlfriend is also going out with another dude buddy of mine and feels "weird" about last night. My grrrlbuddy seems pissed at me for actually jumping in/on her bestest girlfriend. Now I realize I really like her...and her bestest girlfriend. And her other girlfriends are pretty hot. I want to have mouth porn with all of them.

My wife has no idea.

<u>633651531</u>

I was happily married for 24 years when I contracted a STD from my husband. He confessed to a one-night stand with a hitchhiker he picked up when he drank too much. He has been trying to make it up to me ever since but I still bug his car with a recorder to see if it happens again. It hasn't. Now, I let myself get picked up by a strange guy & did it in his truck...and I didn't use protection. I haven't told anyone & I feel worse than I did before...

<u>863798993</u>

I once had two boyfriends at the same time. They never knew about each other. I used to spend the day with one and then the evening with another. Sometimes I would even have sex with both in the same day. I am not proud of it and I feel guilty about it to this day. I've changed a lot since then.

<u>336633528</u>

I happen to believe that you can be deeply in love with someone but have physical relations with other people on the side and that doesn't cheapen your love for the first person. But of course I can only admit that anonymously.

<u>613677455</u>

I have cheated on every boyfriend I've ever had.

<u>567639337</u>

Is it possible to marry someone and have a good marriage after you have cheated on them upwards of 7 times over

7 years and never told them?

I hope so.

311922868

I'd like to think that I wouldn't fuck my best friend's ex. I want to think that I'm a good person and there's some things you just don't do, no matter how tempting.

But I will, the second I get the chance.

562007443

Oh god where do I start. I have been with my boyfriend for almost five years. He is a great guy, thoughtful and sweet. I am pretty sure I love him. The problem is I don't remember the last time we had sex and he has never told me "I love you!!"

As a result I have cheated on him oh I think about 20 times. God I feel like such a whore and I know he would never cheat on me. I don't know why the hell I'm still with him. The only thing I know is that I can't live with out him. I kind of want him around as a spare time and at the same time get it on with any cute guy that comes along. The problem is the guys that I do meet are a hell of lot younger, I mean 6-8 years, and they want to marry me. So not ready for that I'm only 28 so I ditch pronto. Damn why can't my bf pay attention to me! This bites!

585865571

I want him to just bend me over and fuck me already. My boyfriend would never know because he is overseas in Iraq. I stayed out with the guy all night and I woke up late... I didn't even have time to shower this morning. I feel so dirty and just wish he would bend me over already or, at least, try to stick his dick in my mouth, so that things can get awkward and I can dump him soon, before Steve gets back.

549605346

I stalk my friends on AOL Instant Messenger with a secret screen name.

994921058

We teepeed a girl's house but got away with it because her parents thought it was the fault of disgruntled basketball players. She is editor of the school newspaper which wrote a critical expose on the team.

Sometimes it would be nice if timing were a person, so that we could hug it.

525632722

When I was younger, until I was about 16, when I got the shits with my parents I would lock myself in my room and turn off the TV aerial power supply off and leave them TV-less until I felt better. 5 years later I think about it and I still laugh.

373719337

I really liked this guy who was well out of my league. However he seemed to enjoy talking to me. We were at a party in winter, I went to leave, slipped on the icy step and hit my head. I was hurt but ok. I pretended to be completely knocked out so that he could carry me back into the house. It felt good.

262699380

My wife is a good lay, and she thinks I am the best too. But I've found somebody else; our cleaning lady.

831599842

I'm seeing two girls, in somewhat long distance relationships, at the same time now. If I see each of them about half the time one should see a normal girlfriend, they just add up to one, and it's not so wrong... right?

942931399

When I was a law student I drew up a contract transferring the immortal soul of the signatory to me. My colleague and I went to the liquor store and bought a fifth of Gordon's gin. We went out to the park and convinced a homeless guy to sign the contract in exchange for the gin.

I lost the contract a long time ago.

I am an atheist. I have no idea if he was.

210477254

I just found out I've been overpaid $800.

I'm not going to tell my boss I'm going to just keep the money.

510451004

I've been feeding my cat expired cat food.

843367649

My best friend's dad pays child support for my son. I got his wife pregnant before they divorced.

200994943

I told my boyfriend I'd never cheat on him again. Then a guy who hadn't called me in three months asked me to come over. And I did.

426605457

I realize this confession seems trivial compared to others I've read, but it's still meaningful to me:

A few years ago, I really loved a girl that was with another guy but I never told her so. I felt safer having her as a friend rather than risk losing her because I'm terribly insecure and inexperienced.

I made the mistake, however, of confiding my true feelings with my friend.

A week later the three of us went on a trip to California together. She and my friend fell in love and I watched and agonized through every single moment of it. My friend seemingly relished in torturing me with my own inaction and feelings of inferiority and I couldn't escape it.

The next few days became a special kind of agony. I couldn't bear to watch my love fall in love with my friend in front of my eyes. They stopped talking to me, and would go off on their own for hours at a time. I became jealous and filled with rage. And they knew and did nothing.

What I never told either of them, though, was that on the second-to-last day, when we were driving on the cliffs of the Pacific Coast Highway, I was so close — so close to wrenching the wheel to the right and throwing us all into the ocean below that to even think about it and write about it now makes me shudder. I was so close. I don't know what stopped me.

I never spoke to either of them again, but three years later I'm still in love with her and I look her name up on Google. I can't describe how embarrassed I feel to confess that here.

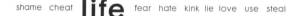

There was one day when I had some bad life. Work was a problem, girls were several problems, and the music that I loved wasn't sympathizing with me. I decided to get very drunk. My roommate wasn't a friend, just a room-mate. There was nothing to drink so I called him, as a roommate, and asked him to pick up some liquor. Vodka, I said.

I dropped in an olive and swallowed. It was warm, entirely dry, and awful. Vodka from a plastic bottle, probably made in Brooklyn. A few more of those and I was barely moving. I became suddenly both loud and tired while my roommate, out of nowhere, became sud-denly and aggressively gay.

"Can I give you a blow job?" he asked.

"No." I tried to let it go as a joke.

"Are you sure? Why not?"

"I'm sure. No fucking way." I thought that would end it but he barely hesitated.

"Will you suck my dick?"

Something about being lit nearly to immobilization made me nervous about this scene. I left the room and ran a bath. He woke me up. I had fallen asleep in the tub and he was taking a piss in the toilet next to my arm.

"Why are you taking a bath in your clothes?"

"I really don't want to see that. Why are you doing that?"

Getting out of hot water, dangerously drunk, in your clothes, is hard. He was starting to get undressed. I was,

*for the first time since Chad the Nazi threatened my life
in freshman algebra, genuinely afraid.*
    "Seriously. Get out of here."
    "I'm going to get in the bath tub."
    "I'm getting out."
    "Fine."
    *I don't remember falling asleep. For unrelated rea-
sons I moved halfway across the country very soon after
and haven't spoken to him since.*

727144448

I just broke down in tears because the hot water wasn't
on and the shower was cold.

I think there's something wrong with me.

126863207

I wish I were a vampire. I know someone else who does
too. She is beautiful and we are almost the same person.
We could sleep all day together then take on the night.
No more drama, no more worries. We can have whatever
we want and get rid of those we don't like. I like plan c.
and I hope you read this.

488108459

My family has so much money they don't know what to
do with it and my mom ends up buying useless things
like ten thousand dollar show dogs that she does nothing
with but let them tear up our house. Sometimes I'd rather
just be poor.

417301935

I normally eat paper.

400211406

I farted quite loudly in church about 2 years ago. It echoed and bounced off all the pews and walls, not to mention it smelled horrendous (a result of biscuits and gravy for breakfast). People wouldn't stop giving my family crap about it, so we had to switch churches, even though my parents liked that church a lot. I don't care, I like our new church better.

472435483

Sometimes I envision a tiny billy goat who keeps watch over my hymen.

175536617

I don't use tampons . . .

or pads . . .

I use bread.

318534578

When I go into sports stores, I always bend the visors of the baseball caps. I hope my actions lessen the amount of people walking around with ridiculous-looking straight visors.

192928062

When I was a kid, I found some beer in the woods that someone had hidden there. I drank two of them and peed in the bottles and put the caps back on. The later that day, my friend called me and invited me to go party in the woods with him and a bunch of other kids, he said they had beer.

526346614

When I was in college and lived in a dorm with a shared bathroom, I was so lazy that I peed in those 20oz soda bottles with the screw-on caps. I had about 15 bottles at the end of the semester. I threw them in the dumpster and continued to move out. As I moved out, I saw an indigent family climb into the dumpster and empty out each bottle to collect the 10 cent deposit fee. The stink could be smelled from over 200 feet away b/c the pee was months old. The family had very depressing looks on their faces, but they needed the money anyway.

769446782

Once I got really, really drunk and before my buddies and I went home, we stopped at Jack in the Box. I bought $27 worth of food for myself, but it was all to go. I crashed over my friends apartment that night and he passed out while I ate and watched TV. I could only eat a fraction of what I got, but I got paranoid that he would wake up and eat it. I snuck into his room and hid it in his closet. Unfortunately I forgot about it in the morning. He found the food about 5 months later and the mold had gotten all over his stuff. He didn't remember that it was my food. It still makes me laugh.

406429093

I have intentionally urinated on someone before.

93916495

I own 7 different guns. My mom has confiscated 3... That fucker.

163993154

All the time I find myself wanting to eat flesh. In public I eat the flesh off the tips of my fingers but at home I eat the soles of my feet the skin is so thick and chewy. I bite myself all over I'm sure I've gotten flesh from every part of my body except my pussy but while I'm getting laid and a guy's eating me out all I think about is how my pussy flesh would taste if he bit a hunk off and gave it to me to chew. I'm not a cannibal, just one motherfucker of a confused chick, I just love the taste of flesh... 17/f

450933231

I eat pills I find on the floor.

979048243

I voted for George [W.] Bush in the last election.

988070868

I hate taking a shit and everything about it. It's time consuming, the buildup's uncomfortable, and it's annoying to clean myself afterwards.

I take Imodium on a regular basis so I only have to poop twice a week.

664049554

I pee in the shower.

I drive drunk.

I pick my nose and sometimes I eat it.

I used to hump my stuffed animals when I was younger. I didn't even know how to masturbate properly, so I would rub up against them and get myself off. It felt incredible, even when people would walk in on me writhing under the covers.

I gave my boss a hummer for $.

I have klepto tendencies.

I love my current boyfriend and have never been unfaithful to anyone, but can't stop thinking about sleeping with my ex. He was hot as hell, had a long thick cock and knew how to turn me on anytime, anyplace. And he enjoyed it. Maybe my sex drive is too high for a female.

I am manic-depressive.

449307741

I like to keep friends who are uglier than me, fatter than me, or dumber than me so I look really good next to them.

699802122

I'm a female and I shave my knuckles.

201043304

I went to a Kenny Rogers concert and he was throwing Frisbees into the audience. He only threw the Frisbees to the women, so I was pissed off I didn't get one. I don't know why. I only went to the concert to hear him sing "The Dukes Of Hazzard" theme song, and he didn't even sing that. That show was such a rip off.

626043128

I stopped reading *Fast Food Nation* half way through because I do enjoy the McDonald's Sausage and Egg Muffin breakfast and, well, ignorance is bliss.

454648560

Well...its kind of hard to say this...I don't know...it was a weird time. Well here's how it goes. I was walking down a street one day and found this muskrat that couldn't walk. So I picked it up and brought it home and started caring for it. I fed it pizza. We watched TV...and I named it Henry. He became my best friend and he died yesterday. I don't want to believe he is dead, **he's still on my chair!** I'm just going to leave him there...

325650418

So constipated.

534015472

My butt is always itchy. Sometimes I go to the bathroom at work just to scratch it. It's not a little scratch either. I scratch right up to the anus. Maybe I have worms.

114781373

I work at a hair salon and I save the hair of a particular woman whose hair I style. I keep the hair in jars that I store in my basement.

359859223

I enjoy getting upset while driving; I love to yell obscenities out my car window. One time I called an old man a "cunt" and he looked at me as though I was Satan driving a Subaru wagon; another time, when a church bus pulled out right in front of me, I screamed "I hate your god!" A couple little kids looked back at me, scared.

752477018

I hate having clothes on. Whenever I am alone, I go topless at a minimum, and if I don't have anywhere to go for a while, I get completely naked, or wear nothing but a robe (without tying it). I never answer my door when someone knocks, even when they know that I'm home, because I don't have any clothes on.

843734074

I'm a popular female celebrity, super famous in the UK, but I want to commit suicide. I hate this life stuck in the public eye with paparazzi constantly trying to get photos. I know I have a family and thousands of fans who will be devastated, but I don't really care.

717241943

I live in a hippie commune with about twenty-five other people; one of these granola and knit sweatshirts kind of places. A few months ago, a new guy wanted to move in, but he had a police record, so my 'mates were against it. I thought he was cool, so I talked it out with the house, and they decided to let him move in.

I don't know what magic this guy's got, but he's slept with just about everybody that I live with. I stopped inviting my ex-girlfriend over, because she wanted to have sex with him, and I didn't know how I would feel about that. I invited another girl over, and within 30 seconds of meeting this guy, she ditched me, and went into his room for the night, never to emerge. This guy has a strict code of promiscuity, and has told me that any girl I bring into the house with me is fair game for him. I'm an attractive guy, and don't have problems getting girls interested in me. But, this guy's sexual charisma is light years ahead of mine, he has no scruples, and I can't compete. It's destroying my sex life.

Sometimes, I want to stick an axe in this guy's face. Not

a very hippie thing to do, but I think that I'd find the sight of blood spurting out of this guy's head to be relaxing. Grind up his guts in a blender and feed it back to his no-animal-products-whatsoever eating ass.

904468066

I still sleep with a teddy bear sometimes.

758432913

I think deep down I believe that I'll be able to trick God into believing that I'm actually a good person when the time comes.

16580231

I feel guilty and sometimes ashamed about how much money my family has and the privileges that has afforded me.

522618055

Once when I was at the cinema I needed to have a piss half way through the film. Because I didn't want to go to the toilet, I pissed in an empty Coke cup and put it in the cup holder on the armrest. It was actually quite a shit film. I don't know why I couldn't just have gone to the toilet and missed a few minutes of the film. But doing the wrong thing gave me a buzz.

399282639

I once was waiting for an elevator and when the doors opened, there was a baby there on the floor of the elevator in the car seat. Instead of taking the baby out, I instead waited for the doors to close and take the baby to another floor.

186791769

A girl at work once whispered to me "come to the paper room so we'd be alone"...I looked at her and asked "why?"

812061834

I just ended a phone conversation with my boss by saying "peace."

183365722

I really wish I was in the witness protection program. Not because I'm in trouble, but because I'd like to start over with a new name, new job, new life. A fresh start.

There should be a company that provides this service.

795032868

I ate two power size doughnuts and two doughnut balls for breakfast.

55623900

I procrastinate like a mutha. I think I'm better than most, and judge people in a holier-than-thou context. I use big words to sound smart. I know I'll be a failure in life, but have this optimistic attitude that I'll be something great, even though I won't work for it. I don't know who I am. I'm too reliant on personas and fronting an image. I'm too easily swayed by information/opinion. I don't have a strong mind of my own. I watch too much porn. I waste too much time.   I plan, but never carry out. I don't have any self-discipline. I dickride so easily. I tell people what they want to hear, or more precisely, what I think they want to hear. I cling onto people I want to get to know, and elitist-ly avoid people I don't want to know. I base my decision to get to know people on superficial factors such as looks, or selfish factors such as how they can help **me**.

394715981

I really like the taste of turkey Gerber baby food.

873966489

Sometimes I wish that I was retarded and act on all my impulses freely.

416433043

I don't believe in god.

139879104

I secretly pray to God just so I have a backup.

383154391

I'm queer and rarely do I find gay men attractive. The majority of them are tacky and queeny. I might as well just flirt with straight men, or date a woman because at least there would be breasts to play with and I wouldn't have to listen to soul divas. Oh, god, why me.

58393391

I slept with one person in my entire life, and got an STD. I guess it's better than a kid.

42863711

I once hit a car with my boyfriend's truck. It was real bad and I didn't leave a note or anything.

I'm really nice to people and sometimes I hate it more than anything.

I just got dumped by my boyfriend and I am on the lookout for a new boyfriend just to make him mad and jealous. I don't even want a new boyfriend.

I smoke and drink and my family has no idea.

My boyfriend told me he was a virgin but I never believed him even though I said I did.

I stole from my work.

I cheated on a boyfriend before.

I am infatuated with someone and I don't even know why.

My friends all suck and when my friends that don't suck call I tell them I'm too busy or I just don't answer the phone.

I've looked at porn before.

Sometimes I wish I had an eating disorder just so I could be skinny.

I'm afraid to go to the doctor cuz I think I might have a tumor.

I swear way too much.

I'm really out of shape.

I call my friend a whore behind her back...but she really is in a big way. Serious.

My parents piss me off and sometimes I wish they would get divorced.

I enjoy watching Jerry Springer.

Sometimes I feel like punching people in the face for no reason.

Sometimes I like crying.

I really want a boob job...no matter how bad I tell everyone I think it is.

I talk shit about everyone...seriously.

I avoid the homeless people who play music on campus for money because it makes me laugh and I feel like sh*t for laughing at them.

I enjoy saying the f word way too much.

I'll probably flip through these thousands of pages after I write this just to read my own sad entry.

I don't like school and I feel really bad because it's really expensive.

Sometimes I want to do really bad stuff but I don't because I'm scared of going to hell.

I'm pretty sure I spit in someone's food once....or dropped it on the floor or something. I dunno, but it was bad.

I always laugh inside when the eye doctor gets in my face with that stupid eye scope.

I make fun of how this old lady at church sings. It really drives me up the wall.

My mom thinks I'm a really good kid and I'm really not....at all.

I once vandalized a high school that was a rival of mine.

Sometimes I pee in the shower.

I get really mad for no reason sometimes.

I like reading stupid shi* like this on the Internet.

I spend way too much time f*ckin around on the computer.

I'm lazy.

I procrastinate.

I'm pretty smart but I let it go to waste.

I eat really unhealthy.

I kissed another girl once. Bad.

I think I'm addicted to diet pills.

My life is quite sad. I should do something about it I suppose. Hm, oh well.

262682896

If I hadn't grown up in society I would want to touch people all the time all over.

129891320

One of my better friends at my university has this habit of petting his sideburns, and I swear to God, if I see him do it again, I'll shave them off.

It drives me nuts.

382049097

I'm in love with this guy who has a super cute girlfriend. I really like her and pretend to be friends with her and whatnot, but I secretly plot to kill her sometimes...one time I was holding her legs up for a kegstand and I tried to figure out a way to drop her on her head so her neck would snap...I wouldn't really do anything. I also imagine running her over with a train, I would be wearing one of those conductor hats and would yell out to her "train's leavin!" then swirv off the tracks and run her ass over...is that even possible? Probably not. But damn that would be sweet.

561268228

Once I sat next to my friend in a hot tub and as she was talking (she is a bitch), I just peed a lot and smiled...a lot.

345542986

I fucking hate eating pomegranates because they're such a god-damned hassle. I used to eat them, and for some reason I stopped. But now, I remember why.
Such a god-damned hassle.

512969375

I majored in sociology, the study of people. But I hate people.

I do like the jargon. But I hate the irony.

688751156

Every time I go to the movie theatre it is overrun with a bunch of "tweens" you know they're not quite teenagers yet, and they are loud as hell.

They run around totally unsupervised with cell phones that flash. I find myself distracted from the movie and fantasizing about tripping them, and rubbing their faces into the ground, and breaking their cell phones. Parents need to watch their damn kids.

300225532

I'm a hot guy trapped in an ugly mans body.

474242878

My ex-boss was putting an employment ad in the paper. She wrote "wizzy-wig" instead of "WYSIWYG" on one of the specs... I didn't bother correcting her.

I thought it was fair warning for anyone applying to the job on how clueless this woman was.

869290568

I am 15-year-old male and am not fat but I have sort of big man boobs. My stomach isn't big though. So if my little boobs are pressed down they look like muscle. So, in conclusion...I wear a female sports-bra my best girl-friend's mom gave me. The bad thing is that I am gay and I love to wear tight clothes. I wear tight shirts and I am so afraid the lines are going to show and I am constantly tugging at it. I am sure by now everyone knows and they probably think I am a cross-dresser...**I'm not!**

754631692

My eye-doctor's heavy breathing creeps me out. I don't think he'll be my eye-doctor any more.

625031247

I like to draw on my body, it relaxes me. I do it in spots where my clothes cover it. People think it is odd that a thirty-year-old male still uses the back of his hand to write reminders and numbers. If they only saw what going on my arms, stomach and legs.

569517147

I'm a 19-year-old male that cries whenever I hear the "Aeris's Theme" from Final Fantasy 7.

164038267

I still like playing with LEGOS.

455826943

I am obsessed with watching how paper towels soak up spilled liquids...it blows my fucking mind.

563352918

My 1-year-old Newfoundland, Todd, loves to hump my wife. I actually get jealous because she laughs and finds it funny or cute. But at that moment all I can see is another male on my territory. How ridiculous is that?

488180794

We used to share baths when we were little, until one day I showed my sister how I could make a fountain of wee. She shouted "mum" and mum made me finish washing my hair in my piss before she ran a clean bath for my sister. I think that might have been when we started having separate baths.

554918579

Back in elementary school we were playing kickball as a class. One guy that I hated had just kicked the ball and was running towards first, admiring his shot when he ran right into the soccer goal post. The resulting "clang" was the best sound I have ever heard in my life, and I burst out laughing. My classmate yelled at me saying "it isn't funny."

Actually, it was. Very much so.

213265320

When I was little, I thought babies came from kissing. It was because I saw the movie *Look Who's Talking,* and they showed two people kissing, then the sperm swimming to the egg, so I guess I just assumed the sperm came from the man's mouth and swam down to the woman's stomach to the egg.

I also used to think that when you get your period, it is permanent (i.e., you just bleed constantly for the rest of your life). Yikes!

969368653

I like to build elaborate forts in my living room and just sit in them for hours on end. I'm 32.

391696933

When I don't feel like explaining my culture or nationality or feel like speaking Korean, I tell people that I am adopted and that's why my English is good.

Also, when I want to bring my own food to the stadium, like rice cakes since hot dogs are too expensive and not tasty like Korean Sushi, and they tell me that I can't, I tell them that I am allergic to eggs and never had a birthday cake in my life which makes them go "Oh... you never had a birthday cake?" and then they let me bring in my food.

117378199

As we speak I'm burning with jealousy because Gabe came up with this website and not me. I'll tell him it's cool, but I hate him for it. I also hate that this'll probably be parlayed into a book and maybe even a movie deal and then I'll just be the guy saying, "Yeah, I knew Gabe when he was just a web-designer with two dead pixels on his screen."

Also, I hate people that write made up shit on this website to entertain themselves. It invalidates everyone else's honest confessions.

365927710

I don't know why, but every time I see someone leave their convertible top down on their car, I have the sudden urge to put something in it. I mean I will rummage through my car to find something to put in there.

The other day I had my fiancé put my iced tea in the cup holder.

One time it was a half eaten peach.

It's a fetish. I don't know where it comes from.

635663605

One of my favorite hobbies is to dress up in designer clothes and do my hair and makeup. Then I put on a baseball cap and sunglasses and go grocery shopping pretending to be a famous celebrity who just wants to lead a normal life.

193128551

Some days I want to kill myself but I want to make it look like my neighbor Ted did it. He won't give me back my lawn mower and I hate him. I hope he gets the chair.

1078988

I pull the nose hairs out of my boogers before I eat them. Because eww; who wants to eat nose hairs?

755640115

I started to become conservative a few years back. I'm better now. I grew out my hair again, I have a long shaggy beard that scares chicks, and I traded in Machiavelli for Locke, but I still feel soiled with greed and corruption.

180146774

When I'm getting ready in the mornings, I like to moan and shudder and squirt out the toothpaste on to my brush as if I'm blowing my load.

146826990

I'm pretty sure I was abducted by aliens when I was younger. I tell people but they think I'm just joking. Sometimes I wake up in the middle of the night with huge pains in my rectum. It can hurt so bad I wanna pass out. I don't tell people that part though.

<u>368963073</u>

It was me who for my muck up day at school in Australia, redirected $30,000 that the school had, in which they were going to use for something they weren't sure of, so they ordered 60,000 pink flamingo grass ornaments to be delivered to the school on the morning of the muck up day, I then made sure that if the school was unhappy with the order that the order was completely refundable, so the school got back the $30,000. It was very well organized. Today it still is the best thing I have ever done!

It was just a sea of pink!

<u>616305961</u>

I have a velvet robe and smoke a pipe with bubbles. I feel unstoppable when I wear it.

<u>529980056</u>

Once, I was listening to a friend's horizontal bop... it made me laugh so hard I crapped my pants.

<u>793815160</u>

I have obsessive-compulsive tendencies.

I have obsessive-compulsive tendencies.

I have obsessive-compulsive tendencies.

I have obsessive-compulsive tendencies.

I have obsessive-compulsive tendencies.

I have obsessive-compulsive tendencies.

I have obsessive-compulsive tendencies.

I have obsessive-compulsive tendencies.

I have obsessive-compulsive tendencies.

I have obsessive-compulsive tendencies.

I have obsessive-compulsive tendencies.

I have obsessive-compulsive tendencies.

I have obsessive-compulsive tendencies.

I have obsessive-compulsive tendencies.

I have obsessive-compulsive tendencies.

I have obsessive-compulsive tendencies.

I have obsessive-compulsive tendencies.

I have obsessive-compulsive tendencies.

I have obsessive-compulsive tendencies.

I have obsessive-compulsive tendencies.

I have obsessive-compulsive tendencies.

I have obsessive-compulsive tendencies.

I have obsessive-compulsive tendencies.

I have obsessive-compulsive tendencies.

163839875

I just farted, but it looks like the girl is asleep, so no harm, no foul, right?

798461257

I've stopped resisting so much. As a result, I find the world less important and more pleasant.

476646139

I worked at Hooters.

750230370

I'm sick of schmoozing with assholes I don't like over cocaine and cocktails.

291497973

I am a girl who *refuses* to shave my moustache off, I feel like it is a part of me — People tell me I look like Tom Selleck.

143731580

When I was younger, I thought if you had braces and glasses then you were so awesome and hot...I was a very jealous little kid.

820642509

I'm 15 and I am a twin with a boy and I live with my dad no mum. All my life I have been brought up as a tomboy. I started going to football when I was 7 and have been eva since. I now am playing for a women's team and I'm actually proud. In school I am very popular which I hate because I'm not popular for me, just the way I look. I have really large boobs and of course 15 year old boys notice this. I have long blonde hair and I'm normal size: not fat, not thin, I have been out with loads of boys and I was very stupid when I was younger and hung about with the wrong people. I take drugs everyday of my life mostly E or cocaine which ever I feel like. I lost my virginity when I was 13 and a drunken MESS and really didn't enjoy it. It was with my dealer at the time. I finished with him after I found out he had been with 2 other girls whilst with me. When I was 14, I'd already had sex with 5 different boys for no reason — just when I was drunk. I lost a lot of my girl mates except for my girls in the team because of drug abuse. I never have smoked a fag but I smoke at least 2 spliffs a day. I love it. I love being stoned. I love not giving a shit about anything! My Confession is...when my brother found out about all this, I denied it all. My dad thinks I am a little angel, so as he threatened me in my room, I decided the only way I could make him not tell my dad is to bribe him back, so I decided to bribe him with the fact that I knew my brother at the age of twelve had sex with my dad's girlfriend at the time! Of course he went mad and we agreed that nothing would be said, then there was a big fight last Christmas and my dad heard us arguing about it. My dad chucked my brother out and now my brother lives in a flat. He went from being the most popular and brainiest kid in our year, to low life scum. He does drugs and drinks constantly. He and my dad were like bread and butter. Of course, my dad chucked me out 2, but I am living with my aunty as my brother refused to ever look at me again. I saw him 3 days ago in the shop. He looked at me and started to cry, and so did I. He then walked out the shop. I don't think I'll ever see him again. I am so sorry for splitting up my family.

758637689

I miss college. I miss working in the sculpture studio and having crushes on other art students. I miss being creative. I miss thinking I could be something instead of knowing I won't be. I miss staying awake 'til 4 AM only because the person I am talking to doesn't want to be alone anymore than I do. I miss being around friends all the time. I miss being excited about the day. I miss that girl I kissed only once but the thought of her still gives me the shakes when I really think about it.

If you see her tell her I said hello.

411691002

I'm crazy but I keep it under wraps. It's not the fun psychotic kind of crazy, either; it's the neurotic woe-is-me personality disordered brand of crazy. Consequently, I can't let people get close to me because they get freaked out when they find out about me.

I'm Fucked Up NOS.* I abuse alcohol, I'm paranoid, I have bulimic behaviors, periods of mania, periods of depression, and a lot of compulsive tendencies, I'm a perfectionist, I'm shy, I'm a narcissist, I bear grudges, "I'm selfish and I'm sad" (and overly fond of chick music!), I'm extremely obsessive and I stalk my exes, I hate my parents, I'm convinced that I'm unlovable and incapable of love, and I'm addicted to this site.

Most of my friends don't know the extent of my craziness. Some of them have an inkling, and they think my issues are cute. Superficially, I'll admit, they are endearing. Boyfriends, however, always end up finding out about my weirdness, especially when we start fooling around. My choice is either to destroy relationships by never letting them get close for fear that they will find me out, or to let them find out and freak out. Ah, well, the end result is the same either way.

*NOS (Not Otherwise Specified) indicates that symptoms do not meet the criteria of a specific disorder (i.e., Anxiety Disorder NOS).

My first boyfriend dumped me when he found out that liquor is my lifeblood, that I was eating only salad that month, and that I have a two-hour morning grooming ritual. After he dumped me I put up all these hysterical away messages and drunk dialed him every weekend night for weeks after. He's so afraid of this crazy girl that he literally leaves the premises whenever we see one another somewhere.

I was going to get together with another guy, but he'd read my Live Journal and knew all about me so he was too freaked out to start a relationship with me. We just hooked up instead.

Then I dated a guy who was crazy in the fun, uninhibited, spontaneous "I'm a sociopath on speed" kind of way. We both thought the relationship would work because we were both nuts; unfortunately, his brand of crazy wasn't the same as mine and things deteriorated. He stopped calling me, and I hired a friend to destroy his car. I spent months brooding and breaking things and being so angry at him that I couldn't see straight. Now I read his and his new girlfriend's Live Journals regularly and create new accounts to leave nasty comments in their blogs.

I have stopped allowing myself to enter relationships, and only hook up from now on, and even **still** I find myself unable to hide all my neuroses and strange compulsions. I'm so tired of apologizing for being nuts. Why can't anyone understand me and not expect me to be a perfect little goody two shoes? Come on, I'm sure I'm a much more interesting person than most girls out there.

994992050

The only woman to ever see my penis is my mom.

I'm 24.

145063300

I spit in someone's shoe becuz I was mad at them but then it turned out that they didn't really do the thing that I thought they did.

Now that person's turned into a rebellious punk and I hope I didn't have anything to do with it.

He never knew I spit in his shoe though.

This Monday me and my mom saw a guy from our "church" walking home with groceries in the pouring rain. We wanted to stop and give him a ride home but didn't have time. He died later that night. I wonder if we could have done anything different so he might still be here. (He was 58 and died of asphyxiation.)

When I was 17 about me and my best friend walked to the convenience store for candy at 2 AM.

When I was even younger than that, me and my other best friend walked to the convenience store really late at night when all the parents had gone to bed.

I have drunk 6 alcoholic beverages in a row and where I come from this is considered binge drinking. I was not drunk though.

531321235

I'm 20 years old, and just figured out that Kanga and Roo from Winnie the Pooh spell out the word "kangaroo"

971568824

Thinking that I just needed some time off from college, I

dropped out. I wanted to get a hold on my life, so that I can figure out who I am as a person. Just take a little time off, make some money by working at the mall, and relax. It seemed right at the time, but it's lost its flavor.

Now, I work at a "tobacco" shop located between a liquor store and a "full-service spa." I took the job for the sophisticated feeling I got when describing a fine cigar to someone. Instead, I sell crack pipes for a living.

I've had nowhere to live since moving out of the dorm, and am currently sleeping on a friend's couch, surrounded by filth and spiders (I've got a terrible case of arachnophobia) in the middle of the ghetto. I would get a gun for protection, but I can neither afford one and am not old enough (19).

Sometimes I dream about what the perfect life would be for me... being married to a girl I know from high school (who's best described as sweet, beautiful, morally strong, intelligent; a. k. a. Perfect); living in a decent house on the beach; having 2 little girls; a job as a writer, not insanely famous but making enough to live comfortably; and every night, sleeping softly with the satisfaction and peace of mind that only very few people experience — the feeling of pure, unconditional contentment.

That is all I want. Instead, as I fall asleep shivering from a broken heater and listening to the sounds of booming rap music, sirens, and the occasional exchange of gunfire, I wonder how I can fix this mess; and if I even can. All I've got to look forward to tomorrow is the possibility of enough gas in my car to get to work and back, and maybe enough cigarettes and vodka left to make me forget my dreams for another night.

C'est la vie. Pass me an ashtray and a shot glass.

835503949

I've always believed in trying everything at least once. I liked anchovies on my pizza. I didn't like getting fucked in the ass by a huge black guy.

815002464

I am horrible.

I once cheated on my ex with the previous girlfriend. I then tried to hook up again with said previous gf, but she wasn't into it. I still dream of fucking her again.

My current girlfriend only turns me on occasionally.

She also annoys me by being overtly sensitive, demanding, nagging, lazy, self-centered, and god knows what else. Sometimes I just want to off her. I don't know if I love her, I tell her I do but I'm not sure.

I also lie to her constantly. Things I didn't do, I tell her I did and then blame something or someone else when nothing happens. Sometimes I don't tell her things that happen, or things I do, and when she find out I pretend to be surprised.

I chock out free porn sites weekly, and jack off every time. Black girls, especially, turn me on. I want to have anal sex with a slim black girl with firm tits and large nipples.

I pretend to be a feminist in front of people to show off, when I fact I don't give a fuck about anyone. Not even myself.

I once slept with my ex-girl while she was asleep. She found out, and I managed to convince her that I thought she was awake.

I want my girlfriend to lose a lot of weight but I can't tell her.

Her mum drives me mad sometimes, she's dominant, demanding, loud, easily angered, self-centered, ignorant and ingratiating.

I have chest pains from time to time, and trouble breathing, but I don't tell my girlfriend or family about it because they just flip out (especially my girlfriend).

My girl wants us to marry, and I pretend I want that too, when in fact I hope that she'll get tired of me and leave me so I won't have to put up with her anymore.

I'm ashamed of my friends, and I wish I had cooler friends so I can be cool too.

Add to this, I'm also ashamed of my heritage and I wish I was someone else.

I can't take criticism. When people criticize me I try to act like I'm all cool and accepting, but in fact I want to saw that person's tongue off with a blunt knife and kick them in the groin. I think everyone who doesn't agree with me is an idiot, and anyone who doesn't understand why I do things should fuck off.

I think my co-workers are idiots, and less intelligent than me. They have no class, no style, no taste, and they're extremely uninteresting. I even hide from one of them when I see him because I think he's such a nerd.

I want to get it on with one of my female co-workers, though.

I like to pretend like I have class and style, but I'm afraid I don't. Again, I wish I was someone else.

I probably have some self-confidence, but no self-respect and self-esteem. I bore myself, and I constantly let myself down.

I'm so tired of living this life, but I won't off myself because suicide is for junkies and bullied people.

397633263

When I'm out running, I secretly feel superior to all of the people who walk by me. I like to believe that they know I'm better than them too.

793929793

I am a lazy sloth. I do as little as possible. I might eat, but only if someone brings it to me. Even so I weigh over three hundred pounds.

My house is a mess, but rather than clean it I look at it, shrug, and walk around the mess. I have paths through the house in spots where there is so much crap piled up that you can't do anything but sidle by. I'm sure it's not only disgusting but a fire hazard.

I'm embarrassed that I live this way, but still I do nothing. My mother won't come to my house and this pleases me. I never allow anyone to come in to visit either. I stand outside and talk to them from the top of my steps and make them stand in my unkempt weed ridden shambles of a lawn. The upside is that I'm never bothered by salesmen anymore.

I sit all day and play on the Internet or with video games. I hate myself. I want to have the energy, and the motivation to get out and do things outside like I did when I was younger, but I seem not to have it, and not likely to get it.

I'm afraid I'm going to die soon, and I feel like no one else around me gives a damn even though they can see it too. How could they miss it? I weigh over three hundred pounds!!!

I am honestly afraid that — in the end — a mildly per-verse Web site and this book might be considered my major contributions.

568436811

I always clean the toilet seats before using it. I have bacteria-phobia.

675098291

I had oral sex 3 years ago with a gay guy who has HIV. Since then, I've had sex with 12 women, 3 without con-doms. I'm afraid to get tested and find out if I'm infected. If I am, there's no way I can track down all the women, let alone have the nerve to call them out of the blue and tell them the horrible news. I'm probably clean, but still too scared to find out.

I'm not gay either, just took too much ecstasy that night, and never hooked up with a guy again after that.

410088153

I am very afraid that I will die someday, and when my parents come to clean out my room, they'll find my vibra-tor and my memory will be tainted forever. Unfortunately, I don't know what to do about this, and I sure as hell am not giving up my vibrator.

415333851

I have herpes. I don't know 100% who I got it from. I had a one-night stand with this guy from school, and then a week and a half later I began dating (and sleeping with) this other guy. I haven't kept in touch with the first guy, but two years later I'm still dating the second one. Anyways, at the time he told me he'd never had a sexually transmitted disease. Never had cold sores or anything. Four months into dating him, I've got all these symptoms. I look up all this information online and I'm pretty sure it's herpes. I tell my boyfriend, he asks to look at it and I show him. He actually laughs and says it couldn't be herpes — he tries to reassure me and says it's nothing, I'll be fine. I go to the doctor and she's sure it IS herpes, runs a bunch of tests to be positive, checking for other STDs as well. She was quite unsympathetic. Very medical. I was 18-years-old and crying naked in her office and she calmly starts telling me that having this puts me at a higher risk for developing AIDS, and if I do have HIV I won't be able to get life insurance. Yeah, life insurance. Which is already at the bottom of a normal teenager's priorities, let alone one with HIV. But I have herpes — the doctor was right, my boyfriend was wrong. (Nothing else came up positive.) My boyfriend gets tested and shows positive as carrying the herpes simplex virus, but we have no idea if he gave it to me or if I had it first and gave it to him. Statistically, he's the one that gave it to me. Even though he's never had any symptoms. Because he hasn't ever had symptoms, he doesn't ever acknowledge that he has this...

I'm worried about breaking up with my boyfriend and meeting someone new. Someone that I'd have to sit down and discuss what herpes is, and how wearing a condom doesn't prevent it from being transmitted (because it's passed through skin contact, not by fluids) and whether he would still want to sleep with me, knowing all the risks. I think morally I'd have to let him decide if I'm worth possibly contracting a disease over. I have so many fears about my future regarding all of this. And I just really wish I had a friend I could talk about this with.

855692379

I have a mitten phobia. Anytime anyone wears knit mittens, and tries to touch my arm or any part of my exposed skin with them, I freak out and run. I just don't like the feeling, and something about the way mittens look creep me out.

586499968

One time, I was walking down the street, and I saw a puppy. He was all skin and bones, and it made me feel guilty to see him go hungry. So I took the puppy home, and named him Champ. This caused a big fight between my girlfriend and I, because she hates dogs. As it usually went in those days, the argument started getting violent, and I threw the puppy. It hit the wall, and died the next day.

Have fun, Champ.

180822324

I feel as though everyone I know loathes me in secret, as if they hang around just to reassure themselves that there is someone is more futile than themselves. On days like these I wish I lived under a rock and had a lobotomy.

426487997

Whenever I call someone on the phone, I write out what I am going to say. If I am alone, I practice saying it before I call, even if it's just something really short and simple.

I even write in some "ums" so it doesn't sound scripted.

Sometimes I write one version for if a person answers and a different version for if I get the voice mail. If I haven't written a voice mail version and I get the voice mail, I have to hang up and call back later after I have written a voice mail version.

When there is a voice mail system that allows you to listen to your message before sending, I usually erase and re-record the message at least 5 times before sending.

808254681

I'm 16, a guy, and afraid to have sex. Don't get me wrong, I'm sure in the right situation I would love it. I don't feel I'm unattractive, and I've had chances before to do it, but I'm constantly afraid that I would be criticized for my size, or bust in no longer than 60 seconds. All my friends have done it, freshmen I know have done it. Most girls I would get with aren't virgins anymore, and that's probably the situation that I would be most comfortable in. Damn.

11727558

Sleeping with just one person forever scares me almost as much as sleeping alone.

435254832

After years of contemplation, I really think that I may be an atheist. It scares me a lot.

429648402

Everyone would tell you I'm the sweetest, most nicest guy that they know, and I think I am, but everyone has a bad side: I'm 19 now (I will try to give accurate dates...but I really don't know) — my parents used to adopt foster children — I was in the 3rd grade — and this girl had to be just a little younger than me — I remember we used to act toward each other in a sexual way, not sex, but maybe dry humping of some sort, I don't think I knew what sex was or what we were even doing, but I know now what ever I did with her was bad.

Unsure of age — around the same time though, maybe 3rd grade, or lower, could have been 1st even, I remember me and my sister would build a tent down stairs out of the cushions on the couch and I guess we would sort of fondle each other, I remember being very interested in the girls part of the body — below the waist — and we would show each other and touch each other, but again, I didn't know of sex or had any idea what we were doing. Sometimes I wonder, if she remembers that, because I can and I wonder if she thinks about it and feels weird to look at me or something, sometimes I want to ask her, but that would just be so weird, like if I told her we did that stuff, and she didn't remember, I couldn't imagine what she would think! She is 21 now. Those things are best left in the past.

I lost my virginity October 5th, 2003 to a girl who has a boyfriend. It was the best sex I have ever had . . . wait, the only sex I have had. I don't feel comfortable with my body and she accepted me for me. I want a relationship with her, but she wont let him go.

I feel I started masturbating at a very young age, likely before the 5th grade, maybe younger, I remember I didn't use to climax since I was young, but it felt good, I can't remember the transition from actually not climaxing to climaxing. At my present age I had always feared that I would not be able to have an orgasm from sex because I was so used to it. When starting young, it would take just my mind to climax, then I couldn't do it anymore, I needed pictures. Pictures didn't work any more, I needed to hear it, then I needed video...I built a tolerance against it I guess. So, just 2 weeks ago I had sex for nearly an hour. My first time, I didn't have an orgasm, but she did 3 times. I don't know if this was good or bad? Stayed up, that's for sure. It really didn't matter to me if I got off or not, I loved just being close to her.

Confessions...hmm, my parents have caught me getting off a number of times, it's the worst feeling.

I have committed credit card fraud many times. I stopped when I almost was caught.

I used to be mean to my pets. I had a little cat and took aggression out on him. To this day, I get a teary eye thinking I did something like that.

My mom thinks I hate her, I love her to death and I'm afraid to show her. I go months without seeing her, and she's 10 min. away.

I have never cheated on a girl, I have came close one time.

I'm not a bad person...am I?

The past cannot be changed.

↖

This story involves a girl we'll call Kate, an old best friend we'll call Tedums, Jack Daniels with lemonade, ten ciga-rettes, and myself. Tedums and I had many a tête-à-tête around the topic of our friendship. Aside from generally being regarded as either blood brothers or "just a couple of fags" among the townsfolk, we usually agreed that we were not best friends. Quite possibly not even friends. We were associates who spent an immoderate amount of time in each other's company discussing film, small fires, and boobies. Tedums had a particular penchant for Kate's boobies, a nice bipolar girl in whom I, too, had a small but rising interest.

Blah blah blah and so we all wound up at a small summer house party. By midnight there had been a minor — and possibly accidental — stabbing on the roof, around back the lawn was on fire, and inside there were murmurs of a missing goldfish and a waterbed lac-eration. I was sitting on the edge of the sidewalk next to Kate, watching Tedums leave, drinking the Jack and lemonade that had just been handed to me. I don't remember if I liked it. I didn't smoke, but Kate did, and I accepted the second lit cigarette that she held toward me. We talked about her ex-boyfriend, her alcoholic parents, and she told me that she used to think I was ugly. Then we kissed.

Tedums offered to pick me up the next day for, I presumed, a typical social outing. Coffee, maybe break-fast. As we left the city limits a half hour later without a word between us, I realized that he was planning to kill me.

The car came to a stop halfway across an 800-foot dam and he got out, walked to the drier side, stepped over the side rail. The drive had taken almost two hours, I hadn't eaten, and I thought I might like to push him over, watch the bastard fall, then — wait, no take his keys, push him over, watch him fall, then drive his old Hyundai to IHOP for a Grand Slam. God was I hungry. I got out of the passenger seat and sat on the hood of his car. I suggested that if he hated me so much then he ought to throw me off of the dam. He said he was thinking about it. We engaged in the stare down of the century on that dam. I think he might have been trying to fake some tears or something, spat something about loyalty and betrayal, demanded to know if I loved her. I probably spat something back about don't be a retard.

Eventually we both got over it, over Kate, and agreed to hate each other as dearest adversaries. It was the defining moment in our friendship. Still, there's this competitive nature even to our casual phone calls.

"Hey Gabe, it's Tedums, what's new man?"

"Tedums! Good to hear from you, I swear I just had my finger on the dial to call you."

"Oh? Looks like I beat you to it."

"Huh. Yeah. Hey, remember that Web site I started? I have a book coming out about it."

"Wow, that sounds neat. I just got promoted."

"I'm going to be on NPR."

"I just got promoted again while you were saying NPR."

"Promoted to what, even bigger liar?"

"No, promoted to I'm Going to Kick Your Ass."

"She didn't want to date you, man!"

"I have more sex with more people and I make more than you!"

Click.

650095414

I'm 19 now. When I was young, maybe around 18, I used to put on a ski mask, gloves, a long-sleeved t-shirt, jeans, socks, underwear, and boots, and go out into my backyard to kill bees. I would go over to my mom's lavender bushes and clap my hands on the bees for about an hour every day.

God I hate bees.

484547006

I live with three other girls. I like one of them and want the other two to die. I dream of axe murderers breaking down the door and them dying. They are fat slobs who just eat bacon and sound like elephants.

100724235

I'm afraid that my guy friends make me look bad. I can't help but get the feeling that any time we go anywhere together, any women we meet would look at me, then look at them, and then decide not to bother looking at me again. I hate them for it.

165694495

I hate the colour pink — salmony pink probably the worst.

699510535

I hate my ex-best friend's girlfriend. I hate high school drama. I hate taking tests. I hate working. I hate having to pay bills. I hate how marijuana is illegal. I hate people who screw other people's lives over to get a point across/or because they can (*cough* U.S. gov. throwing nless pot smokers in jail). I hate rich people. I hate greedy people.

I love sex. I love marijuana. I love women. I love learning. I love winning. I love games. I love Cocoa Krispies. I love hating cigarettes. I love glancing (at breasts). I love knowing I have the power to do anything and everything I want, but I choose not to. I love life.

572359945

I wish that Dr. Phil would kill himself. That would really fuck up the Dr. Phil crowd.

414852481

My boyfriend's dog ate 3 pairs of my panties, some socks, mittens, a stuffed kitten, my boots, and my bra. I hope she chokes on the next thing eats and then she dies. I don't hate animals, I just hate this dog.

714537714

I don't like most people. I think mostly they are stupid, selfish, lame, boring, and ugly. Which is pretty much what I am. But still.

274232014

I hate him for contacting me like that, after so long. But I kind of hope he contacts me again because he makes my heart thump.

602623850

I dumped my boyfriend over the weekend. I should have done it earlier but I wanted to see what he would get me for Christmas.

113645066

I can't tell my girlfriend that I love her. I really do love her even if it took me 3 years to realize. But for the last year I am pretty sure about this and maybe also where it might lead us together. I sometimes hate myself for not being able to tell her.

918256637

I'm jealous of her, that's why we aren't friends.

322617802

This is more a call for one of my roommates to confess something.

So there was a piece of shit on the floor in our bathroom and I know one of you did it.

If no one comes forward there will be disastrous and fecal repercussions.

231367463

When I heard about the child-molesting priest being killed in prison, I was glad. I thought he deserved it. I don't think that it's justice, to kill somcone, but I was still glad and I hoped he was terrified.

722351789

I had an affair with a woman that was intense and passionate. Because I would not leave my wife, however, she became extremely cold and distant to me, and stopped returning my calls and emails. This was several years ago. I have recently found out through third parties that she has lost her job and apartment. Though I confess to still having strong feelings for her, I am nevertheless taking delight in her misfortune. I am a terrible human being.

108545348

I dated this guy and completely fell in love with him...he then dumped me for this fat, ugly, stupid, slutty girl on my soccer team. Needless to say I'm **very** mad and plotting to kill her...

735693892

I hate Rachel because she didn't give me a massage.

262849957

My parents hate my neighbour because he's broken their car and is rude to them. I sneak out my window almost every weekend to have sex with him and come back before they get up.

943777128

When I was 14, I knocked out my older brother's teeth with a pair of brass knuckles.

124623272

I hate my roommate so I had my boyfriend fart on her teddy bear.

108720580

I have no faith in the human race. My job is in tech support. Those stories about people using their CD-ROM drives as cup holders and not knowing where the "any" key is are true. By true I mean one of these happens to me on a **daily basis**. One out of 20 people I talk to has to be told how to type the "@" symbol in their e-mail address, or how to shut down their computer. I had to explain to one guy what an electrical outlet was. Do you know what this means?? This means that an average of 5% of the population barely has the knowledge to get out of bed in the morning. I get paid 7 dollars an hour, and sometimes I get calls from network administrators at companies like Hewlett Packard. I am not kidding. This is not a joke. The world lays in the hands of complete morons.

975920469

Now my wife is on the phone blabbing to someone else. She's so fucking loud. Other people beep in on call waiting and she just tells the same stupid story to everyone.

The talking never stops. It's like she's a machine. Like a version of the terminator that talks instead of killin' folks.

506548433

There is a guy in the office who always, without fail, gives me the shooter salute and clicks his cheeks while winking, I would liko to onop off **his** fingei.

977566727

I scrubbed the bathroom for two hours and my mom yelled at me for not washing the crevices around the sink faucet well enough. I used her toothbrush to finish the job. It gave me a good feeling every time she used the toothbrush, and I wouldn't be averse to doing it again.

449930140

I just broke the paper towel holder in the break room.

I dropped a plastic knife on the floor and then placed it back in the box.

798663747

Sometimes at night I get urges to put a pillow over my roommate's face until his breath runs out, just like in *One Flew Over the Cuckoo's Nest.* I mean, my roommate's a good guy and all, but it's just that movie is sooo rad!

629687923

I thoroughly enjoy the fact that my ex-boyfriend, who dumped me, cannot get over me. He thinks I am the one who got away and I know he regrets everything. He tries to stay in touch and emails me his new information when he moves, like I give a shit what his new phone number is. I don't answer his emails nor do I call him. I have no desire to ever see or speak to him again. He was a horrible boyfriend and brought me such misery. He also dumped me in a very rude and passive-aggressive way . . . I was very hurt. It's ironic that now he is the one suffering and I have moved on with my life. What goes around, comes around. It gives me pleasure that he has "what might have been" on his conscious and I do not.

264815626

Today I yelled so much at a homeless woman she cried.

290462741

I took a shit in the pot plant in the boss's office.

364664749

When my friend plays video games against the computer, I root for the computer.

645598619

One time my friend got really drunk and passed out on the sofa. He had pissed me off earlier so I farted in his open mouth while he was passed out. He deserved it.

511958286

Once my friend's dad was beating his wife, so we peed in his mouthwash, and crapped in the tank of his toilet.

A kid I didn't like in high school used to rant and rave about his car all of the time, so I wrapped his car from top to bottom with 3 rolls of duct tape.

A science teacher in high school kicked me out of class, when I started walking out, he grabbed me by my shirt, so I pulled him hard enough that he fell down a flight of stairs.

I threw a 2 liter bottle full of piss at a group of hippies when I was 15, just because they were hippies.

I stole thousands of dollars worth of videos from a video store I used to work at.

I've had sex in a church.

I've been in a church tripping on acid.

I threw a desk at a substitute teacher.

I punched a girl in the face.

I got in a fight and beat this guy up really bad, when his dad came out to break it up, me and my friends beat his dad up too.

Me and probably about 15 of my friends beat a kid till he was unconscious, later we found out that he was in the hospital for over a week, and had reconstructive surgery. He deserved it though, 5 of my friends were arrested for it.

I don't feel bad about any of it at all.

535221899

I recently bought a new car. I have been saving up for ages. I doubled my working week and got a night shift at Tesco's. It's a really nice K reg Nissan and I loved it.

I went into town one day to meet a friend and hang out. I parked in the local car park where it wasn't busy on a Wednesday lunch. My friend pulls up in the space next to mine in a brand new Peugot 206. I secretly am in love with this car, which is why it hurts so much. On our way into the centre, I slyly keyed the side of his car. It was the whole length of the passenger door.

The next day I found myself in the car park at Tesco's just before I was supposed to be working. I see a relatively new Golf GTi. I could not help it but scratch the car again, this time along the whole car.

I have no regrets except for the fact that I am 39 and 40 in one month and I haven't keyed more things in the past — be them cars or not.

651119810

I can't stand people named Melissa. They are all the same.

924615337

Last night I decided that I wasn't going to stop by a bar on the way home from work as I always normally do. It was the first of the month and I was determined to turn over a new leaf.

I got home all proud of myself and happy, expecting to be met by a loving family. Before I had even taken off my jacket, my wife started shouting at me about where I'd been!! At work — damn it! She went on and on about the laundry and the dishes and the kids, etc., etc., so I just turned around, walked back out and went to the nearest bar and had two beers, two vodkas and a bourbon.

So much for my "new start."

905290565

I have fat aggression.

934961256

I hate artists but wish I could paint.

666952566

I hate "sensitive" guys that try to understand women. It's very unattractive.

326545389

I hate flies. A day that starts with killing one is a good day. As a child I tore their wings off, and liked seeing them that way. Sometimes I have sex with my husband so he'll shut up, go to sleep, and leave me alone.

74120795

I hate George W. Bush more than just about anyone on earth because he's so fucking stupid and is screwing up the world...but I secretly think he's kind of cute.

323273283

One time when I was really drunk I came to my dorm room and deleted all of my roommate's files on his computer because I hated him. He never even suspected that it was me after I told him it was probably a virus that did it. I never felt bad even when he had to rewrite a 5 page paper for his class.

981562063

I want to get beaten within inches of my life. I want to beat somebody else within inches of their life. Just so I know that I am real.

525488560

I groped this girl when me and my guy friends went camping one year. She pushed my hands away from her a few times, but I was drunk, and wanted to show off, so I persisted for a while. I feel like shit. What right do I have? I'm just glad I had the wherewithal to stop myself before going too far. I don't think anyone would have stopped me were I too drunk to stop myself. This is more a confession of what might have been than what actually happened, though what actually happened probably sent me to a worse part of hell on its own merit...

751213806

I'm 16. When I was little I used to catch birds with my bare hands. My grandma says I'd follow them for hours, until they got used to me being there, then I'd pounce on them. I never meant to hurt them, but I killed a couple.

116554296

I'm a police officer, and also a racist.

My friend and I used to go canoeing all the time. We'd catch turtles and baby ducks and geese. Once I jumped onto these rich people's property because baby geese were there. I told my friend to grab one and I'd take care of the mom goose. It got close, so I smacked it in the head with a canoe oar. I was about 14 then.

Yesterday my parakeet that my dad was completely obsessed with died. And I swear to God I didn't touch it.

740589248

My dad verbally assaults my mom, brother, sister, and I every day. When I was smaller (12 and younger), he would ask me if I wanted to go outside and solve the problem like a man, and of course I was too little and said no. Now that I'm much bigger, and could take him on, he threatens to call the police, which he did once on Easter Sunday. He is the one who antagonizes me, why wouldn't he get sent to jail and not me? My mom won't divorce him because he is worth millions, and when I was 10, my family told me that I should get rid of him because I was going no where in life. Sometimes I feel like I should get rid of him, but I don't want to go to prison, for something involving him. He's an alcoholic. Everyday for the past 30 years, he has had a drink. Why did I have to be born into this family? Money fixes nothing, all I want is a happy family. The only thing I have learned from him is hate. I hate him and I hate the local police for taking the side of a worthless drunk. (Folsom, CA)

414900089

I once killed a homeless man with some of my friends when I was a kid. I got five years in juvie for my part in it and then my record was cleared when I became 18.

I wish I was a kid so I could get away with killing people. You'd think I'd feel guilty but I don't. The way I look at it, society decided that five years is a fair trade for some bum's life. I killed him, did my five years, everything is even-steven.

Hell, if all I had to worry about for getting caught was 5 years I'd be out killing a whole shit-load of people. It's not fair that you can kill people and get away with a light penalty as a kid but not as an adult. The fact that I was a kid didn't make that bum any less dead.

I just don't understand how the rules are made. It just doesn't make sense.

441293876

In France I got sick of people jumping my queue, and finally lost it with an old guy who inserted himself slowly 2 places in front of me very slowly. I yelled at him, humiliated him in front of everyone, insulting him (all this in decent French) very strongly, and wouldn't listen to his pathetic attempts to explain...that he was blind and unable to see anything more than a few inches in front of his face. Which is why he was hanging around where he thought the line ended.

695109167

When Dad used to drink too much he would beat up me and my little sister. Mom, she would hide in the bathroom because she knew her licks were coming next. I can distinctly remember the sweet smell of Southern Comfort on Dad's breath when he would come into my bedroom. Knowing that the possibility of a lashing was always there, I would pretend to be asleep.

If Dad was in a good mood he would sometimes kiss me on the cheek and tiptoe out of the room. But on bad nights, I could expect the hissing sound of a belt being slid from polyester loops and the forthcoming sting of leather. Sometimes he used the buckle.

Two years ago, my younger sister and me were talking about our childhood over our own bottle of Southern Comfort. We kept drinking and drinking until our remembrances became focused on those beatings. Dad had never been confronted.

Although we live only a town away from our father, after our mother's passing, we rarely see him. He's a sad old man with only a lifetime of destruction behind him and a future of regrets. That night, my sister and I, drunk as otters, went to see Dad.

My sister rang his doorbell. It was past midnight and Dad answered the door in tighty-whities and a loose robe. He was half-asleep and confused.

I punched him in the face. He crumpled to the floor-boards of the dirty porch with a gasp. My sister and I rained the blows down upon him with a ferocity that surprised even us. In his heart, I know he understood.

583041941

I am a 34yr old single mother who has been raising my son on my own during the last ten years. During that time, I had no time for dating trying to support my son and myself. It has been 10yrs since I have had sex. But lately I have become hypersexual. Everything seems to turn me on. Men that I wouldn't be in the least interested in excite me just thinking what they might have in their pants.

It has been really hard and I have managed to stave off temptation by refusing to go out with anyone. So now I have the reputation of being an ice queen.

I am afraid of giving into temptation and doing something desperate. But I feel that my son might feel neglected or lose respect for me.

<u>231668181</u>

Many years ago, I was part of some computer BBS* club where we all decided to attack one member of our club we didn't like. We didn't beat him up, no, we played with his head real bad. One of us was a psych major, one of us was a reporter, and one of us was a lawyer and we spent many nights drinking and dreaming up shit that would drive him crazy, and between all of our skills, we had a lot of resources. We wrote him anonymous letters, claiming to be his other friends, and saying that we thought he was crazy. He'd come back with the letters, and we'd say we'd look at them, and then "lost" them, claiming we had no idea what he was talking about. We'd send e-mail to his friends, pretending to be other friends, all trying to get them to fight with each other. When he got a job, we'd call his boss, pretend to be a customer, and complain he was harassing us. I think we got him fired once.

Towards the end, he pretty much knew it was us, and although we claimed we knew nothing about his "para-

*Bulletin Board System.

noid delusions" it only made us try and do more shit to him. We knew he was neurotic, and so we attacked his self-confidence over and over. We got a sick joy out of seeing him flip out. We'd send him fake bill collector letters and phone calls, because we knew he was poor (hell, we were responsible for it in many cases!). We even would steal his mail randomly, especially personal letters and bills. We signed him up for magazines, porn, and all kinds of disgusting things, and we'd send them in his name, but to his neighbors' address, so they all thought he was a pervert. Once, we showed up to his workplace, claiming he owed us a drug shipment, and we were going to kill him when he came out. We got a friend we knew but he didn't to harass him at crowded bus stops, claiming he was sleeping with his girlfriend. We even tried to get his wife to leave him by sending her fake tips he was cheating on her, but she was pretty wise to it.

God, we hated that guy. We really hated when he got a break, it was like we had to keep him down to feel good. We loved doing shit with his head! I don't even remember why we hated him now, all I remember was focusing on how fat and stupid and weird he was. We ruined many, many years of his life, and drove him so crazy, he started cutting himself with knives and shit. Then he got wise to one of our dumber participants, and the law got involved, so to this day, we have always claimed our innocence to avoid any prosecution.

I feel real bad about it now. I am not friends with those guys anymore, and that guy we hated is now doing really well as a mystery writer. I bet we fueled a lot of his stories.

Sorry, dude. What can I say? I was messed up.

856852977

When I was sixteen I was driving my parents' car home from brunch after church. For whatever reason we'd decided to eat at a restaurant miles away from the town in which we live, and, as the trip was longish and everyone had eaten more than anyone should, soon after we started home both my sisters and my mom and dad fell asleep. I was a terrible driver and was especially bad in my parents' car, which was a big old baby blue Cadillac. I passed a semi truck w/o enough room and nearly hit another semi head-on (the driver had to pull off the road). I've never told my family that I nearly killed all of us. At least we'd just been to church, though.

596545787

At around age 1 1/2, I've been told that I was busted, not once, but twice, sucking and chewing on slugs from my mom's garden.

467357274

I tripped a mentally ill kid.

371642006

I watched my father murder someone and no one knows I saw it happen, not even him.

146792391

I once got a ride home from a party with two guys who decided to rape me along the way. I still have a scar on the side of my temple from my head being slammed against the window in the backseat. The confession part is that a part of me (just a tiny part) responded. I sometimes can't live with that.

342797236

There was this slow kid at our bus stop. I used to stand behind him and spit in his hair.

579266971

When I was about 8 I was at Sefton Park Lake in Liverpool in England. We were throwing stones at the swans in the lake. None of us really intended to hit one, well I certainly didn't. But I did hit one, right on the head and it died instantly. I ran home crying and have never really forgiven myself.

816786549

During the riot outside of Staples center when the Los Angeles Lakers won the NBA Championship, I threw a glass bottle into the crowd, Soon after I went into the general direction of where I threw the bottle and saw a woman laid out on the floor crying and bleeding from her forehead with glass surrounding her...

603035489

I'm so sick of this. I, of course, was the bigger person and apologized first and all she has to say is "ok." I get nothing in return. The bitch stole my boyfriend, and I forgave her. What more does she want? Why do I have to justify my actions? I didn't do anything. She is heartless and when he hurts her I'll be the first person she runs to. And maybe this time I won't be here for her.

940281357

I press the "door close" button on the elevator when I see people running for it.

857713516

I was in my backyard once and I had my slingshot. I saw a bird in my mom's garden so I walked over towards it with horrible intentions. As I neared it the bird did not fly away, it merely scampered a short distant. I shot my slingshot at it and hit it in the spine with a steel bb. It fumbled around a bit then got it's wings caught in a plant and it's movements faded out of existence. I got a latex glove, picked it up, and put it in a hole in my mom's garden.

Two months later I dug it up to look for bones and stuff. I found some and played with them. Then I put them back and I never go in my backyard except to mow the lawn.

726365375

I lived next door to a deaf kid when I was 14. Every Saturday at like 7 in the morning, he'd go in his backyard and beat on a metal pole with a baseball bat. After 2 months, I had had enough, so I jumped the fence and kicked his ass.

922096479

I used to catch flies in a plastic bag, freeze them into deep sleep, then super glue their feet to post-it notes airplanes. Watched as they woke up and the planes flew away....

499887066

I remember walking home from junior high when a blue Chevy Nova pulled up beside me. A guy in a varsity jacket jumped out of the passenger side and started shouting at me. He kept shouting, "What did you say to me? What did you say?" and I kept shouting back, fearfully, "I didn't say anything! I don't even know you!" He walked up to me and broke my nose with a surprise punch, got back into the car, and the car sped away.

I asked around and found the name of a senior that fit his description and often rode in his buddy's Nova. I sat in the bushes across from his house for a few weeks and logged every entrance and exit. One night, I broke the black plastic at the base of a light bulb, filled it halfway with kerosene, and plugged the hole with a ball of wax. I sliced my finger on the broken base and felt the sting of spilled kerosene.

I broke into his house when he was riding around and replaced the bulb in his desk lamp with my modified bulb. Two days later his picture was in the paper next to an article about him spending the next month in the burn unit.

I still have the article in a shoebox under my bed. Sometimes I worry that without something tangible to keep things straight, the story will alter itself in my mind and become something else.

581825598

I punched an old lady, and broke her nose. She was 94 years old. I didn't **want** to, or even **mean** to. She just said something that really upset me. So I punched her in the face. Now I have to go to court. This is kind of scary for me.

878674118

Once, I checked a Glock and some 9mm ammo out of the RMP* armoury, and then sat outside my ex wife's house

*Royal Mounted Police.

in my car, with the Glock in the glove box, I only wanted to put bits of me in bits of her, but she wouldn't listen, and I think she called the police. Later a policeman came, I flashed my RMP identification but he thought it was a phony cause I'm a fat guy, and he searched the car and found the Glock, I was dishonourably discharged from the RMP.

I also worry about the size of my willy.

57002981

One time I pissed off a 5 story roof onto a couple that was making out on the sidewalk below. I was very drunk but I always felt guilty about that.

593505996

I killed a mouse once by throwing it into a campfire and kicking it back in whenever it tried to run out.

823898394

When I'm tired and cranky and in need of a juice box, I lash out at people with my intelligence, like a condescending jackass

429758485

As a kindergartner, I hoped that the boy who chewed on electrical cords would chew a little harder.

220965176

I was picked on a lot at school, but that didn't matter because I had a good friend that stood by me, until he became a shallow fuck and ditched me for the D&D butter trolls in library. After that happened I started sneaking in his house every Friday night when he was playing D&D with his "friends" and masturbate on his bed.

855516227

I hit my child three times after she declined to make her homework and responding by calling me the worst dad.

I never felt so bad about anything before.

I have a tummy fixation. Tummy-mania.

<u>434562712</u>

When I was younger, me (girl) and one of my girlfriends used to get naked in her closet and lie on top of each other and pretend we were having sex. We were too young to actually know how to do it, so we just improvised. She is one of my best friends today, but we never ever talk about it. Sometimes I wonder if she even remembers.

<u>442151475</u>

My boyfriend used one of his mom's dildos on me. In her bed.

<u>325319493</u>

I write really, really horrible gay fan fiction about the X-Men. Literally, I write homosexual fan fiction about Wolverine having sex with as many male characters as possible, and it's really poorly written.

And my brother helps me write some of it.

<u>755890792</u>

I eat my own cum after masturbating, every single time.

450823025

When I was 8, I'd stay over my neighbor's house 'cause she had a grandson that I'd play with. One night I slept over with him and his two older sisters (13 & 14) were babysitting us. They knew me well from staying over my friend's house and how I was a dead sleeper. When we went to sleep, we all slept on the floor. I was just falling asleep when I heard footsteps and it turned out to be my friend's sisters moving to lay down next to us so I was in between the both of them. I never opened my eyes but I could smell them. In a couple of minutes they started moving and poking me. I kept faking I was asleep. All of a sudden, one of them slid their hands under my shirt and started to caress my chest. I didn't move but it was probably too dark to see me blush. Next thing I know, from the other side of me, the other sister put her leg on me...and since I held perfectly still, she started grinding my leg. Then I felt the other sister's hand slide down out of my shirt, into my pajama pants and under my underwear. The one sister who was grinding my leg started to moan louder and louder that it woke up their brother. I heard him say, "What are you guys doing to __?" Then the one who had her hand in my pants got up and I peeked to see the older sister take him to the other room and tell him something that sounded like, "Just playing a game we made up..." or something and she said not to tell and he agreed to. All the while the younger sister was still getting off on grinding against me...when they finally came back she stopped and though it took me a long time to fall asleep, I did. Now I regret not waking up when they were poking me. I have this problem with being touched now. I'm glad I got that off my chest.

3993042

I have a bizarre kink — I love it when my husband drinks a large amount of water, holds it 'til he really has to go, then pisses hard on my clitoris. It feels amazing.

936493119

I like to look at my friend's breasts.

951257987

I wear a cowboy hat to work just to try and get this girl to suck my willy.

510664809

I once put the "spike" of a spindle of CDs base up my ass. It felt pretty good. I only did it once, and by once I mean twice.

974768722

I've had a problem for years that's changed my life and my jobs all gravitate to it.

I love women's shoes, high heels drive me wild and I'd rather spend a night with a chick's shoes than with her!

I got a job as a meter reader just so I could get into women's houses when they weren't home and get to their wardrobes and wear their shoes, lick them all over and finally jack off in them. I must have done this 100's of times and it gives me a real thrill to think that there are so many ladies out there (ones I'd never be able to go out with) that are slipping on their shoes that have my dried cum on and in them. I've never been caught but worry all the time about it and have tried to stop but I can't!

I guess I'll end up either being caught out or have to quit this job, but then I'd probably end up working in a shoe store where I can help chicks try on hot shoes.

I know I'm weird but the need to want to have women's shoes is sooo strong I can't control it!

<u>625843099</u>

I am 16 and have never kissed. Kind of like the movie *Never Been Kissed*. I want to keep my kiss for someone whom I think I love and who at least seems to love me. I've had one boyfriend who was too nervous to even hold my hand. But I am a teenager and I do get horny. So I started cybering when I was 14. It feels great to lie to these people of various ages. I say my real age and what I look like and I don't care if they are lying because I never do the things I say I do anyways.

Lately though people have gotten a lot more needy. They want mics and cams... I have neither. Without them it's harder to find a cybering partner.

But one day I start talking to a guy when I wasn't looking for someone to cyber with. He was very nice and showed me his cam; honestly, he's not that great looking but I continued to talk to him. (I'm not that shallow. Hell, I have bad taste.) He also lives in the city next to mine when he found out he kept hinting about meeting and after talking to him for a week I agreed. He picked me up and we talked about random things until 3 AM in the car in a parking lot... I didn't even remember he was 22 yrs old until he told me. Usually I would have thought it over but that night I didn't really care.

So as time passed I started drawing on the steam on the window on his side and being hyper because it was so late. He didn't want me to and I ended up with my head on his chest and my hands in his lap. He got hard and me being rather "innocent" I didn't realize this until he had his hands rubbing my back and butt and when he moved my hand on top off it. Then he took off his sweats. I didn't know what to do and said so but gave it a few rubs. It was interesting to finally feel/see one. I felt dirty for doing this with someone I didn't know but when it's late my judgment is pretty bad and it was an awesome rush.

When he found out I've never been "pleasured" he proceeded to do so. I was so nervous but it felt so good. If you remember your first time being touched then maybe you'll know how I felt. I know he's done it before so maybe I was lucky and got an experienced guy. Seriously, thinking about it makes me happy and horny but a feeling of guilt and...dirtiness lingers. So I touched him, he touched me. I might go hang out with him again.

The weird thing is I wouldn't let him kiss me. He seemed kind of put off about it but I've been so persistent in my need to keep my kiss that I moved away when he tried a few times.

Maybe I'm crazy and I don't want to have sex but I do want to "play" again. A confession that only three people know about (me him and my friend who isn't a virgin) is now online. I'm getting gutsy. (Ha ha.)

475447178

I fantasize about having tuberculosis. Every time I cough, I check for blood. It's so sexy and I know I would have lots of attention if I had TB. One day I think I might find someone with it and hang around them a lot until I get it too. It's such a sexy disease.

132848064

Often when I have an important business meeting I wear ladies panties under my suit. It makes me so horny, that I sometimes have to go into the restroom and masturbate (often more than once). I am worried that there might be something in the Bible forbidding this, and that I will go straight to hell as a result. But I don't care, I love wearing ladies panties.

748852934

I have been practicing yoga for two years so that I can suck my own dick. I'm soo close.

284978120

I was baking cookies in the oven, nude. When I bent over to pick up the tray my testicles fell onto the cookie sheet.

I can no longer achieve orgasm unless I feel extreme heat but I told everyone it was because of cancer.

I feel so bad.

374075451

I can't last long in bed.

246363827

I want Tom and I need a drink, enough said.

855269394

My mother had an old "massaging device" when I was little. I thought it was just a back massager. It wasn't shaped like a penis or anything. It just had this big motor with a shaft sticking out of it which was a little wider than my thumb (I have big hands) and about 4 inches long. I'd turn it on and hold it very tightly, trying to make it hold still. Sometimes, I'd stick it in my mouth and clench my teeth on it. I liked how it vibrated my head.

About 10 years later, I suddenly remembered that "massaging device." OMG... my mother had a dildo-like device, left it out all the time, and let me chew on it.

929236206

I was putting a computer together for my boss, and when I was done, I transferred over all his files from his old computer. I then made sure all of his programs worked, including the image viewer. I went to his documents folder, and opened the first picture I found. The picture just happened to be of him with a hooker's hand up his ass. I know it was him, and I know it was not his wife. I became extremely freaked out, and to this day, I cannot look him in his eye. He is an upstanding member of his church, our city, and is always making himself out to be a perfect, moral person. Hypocrite.

349242717

A few nights ago I was out at a bar for Happy Hour with friends from work. I came alone, and by the end of the night there were only three of us. One co-worker brought a cute blond friend with him whom he had met a few months earlier at a train station. I was left with the dilemma of driving them both home, even though I had been drinking. He wanted to go downtown to catch the train and she lived up the street. I wasn't about to drive all the way downtown in my condition and she didn't want the guy at her place. He gave in and we dropped him on the corner so he could catch a cab. I drove the girl home and we hooked up for hours. The other guy, my co-worker, spent the night at Union Station until the trains started running again.

471953814

Not too long ago, I bought a 40 of Capt Morgan, and got completely shit-faced...I proceeded to look at porn on the net and I got all dressed up in drag (make up, hose, 5" heels, lace panties etc...) After I masturbated, I passed out, and my girlfriend found me in the morning.

We haven't talked about it since, and I've thrown all my "girl" things out...I wish I was a girl, and I wish I didn't throw everything away...

I feel like total crap all the time...

899156770

I was at a club one time and wound up making out for hours with a girl who told me she was 17 (I was 19 at the time). Unfortunately, I'm pretty sure she was really 14.

I don't know whether to be ashamed or proud.

952061919

My tastes in pornography are becoming less and less socially acceptable.

673312966

One time, I made a video of myself masturbating, and then I masturbated to the video of myself masturbating.

442765667

I used to get off listening in on my flat mate having sex (with her ex mostly and once with some random guy she picked up drunk) and a couple of times I heard her masturbating (she was a "moaner" and a "sigher"). She liked to make a lot of noise, work the mattress springs, that kind of thing. I'd go to a lot of trouble to keep myself awake nights (she worked late in a bar), be home when she was going to bed (I cut short a date once), just in the hope I'd hear her. I'd come out of a relationship prior to this and when I had a gf, had never paid much attention to my flat mate's "wailing", in fact I found it a turn off. But following my split, I developed a hopeless infatuation with my flat mate which never went anywhere. I don't know, I look back and feel a little sick about what I did but she seemed to want the world to know — the walls were thin but not paper-thin. It was almost like a performance. It turned me on. I've lost contact with her now, I moved away, the idea of doing something like that now creeps me out, but it probably did before I first "listened in." She was great though, you know I look at porn on the net hoping she'll turn up in some pics. Utterly futile. She's a nice girl, I'm sick.

957645445

I once watched my mum get dressed by putting strategically placed mirrors throughout the corridor all the way to my room.

206170747

I met a man on the train today, and went out for coffee with him, let him buy me three drinks, and went back to his place to take a "nap." We fooled around. He's 34, I'm 19.

934065567

I'm 17 and I've always fooled around with my sister, she's 16. It started out when we were little our one uncle used to baby sit us a lot when our parents went out and he molested us, eventually my parents found out and stopped it, but two years later we started doing things on our own.

I get really jealous when she goes out with guys. She likes

me to be with other girls, she even invites girls over and plays truth or dare so she can dare them to kiss me or run into my room naked.

We have sex at least once a week, usually a lot more. We don't use a condom, but she's been on the pill now a year (for other reasons). Sometimes we get really deviant, the other night she let me do anal, even though she didn't really want to. We videotape it sometimes and make our own pornos.

Our rooms are connected to the same bathroom, so at night we lock our doors and she sneaks in to sleep with me. I love just holding her and kissing her. I love her so much and don't want to be with anyone else. She's very attractive and very popular and lots of guys are always asking her out. She says she'll come live with me she gets done high school, my father has a lot of money and has said he would pay for me to get my own apartment.

We had sex once in an airplane bathroom and last week at our family reunion we did it three times, once with two of cousins sleeping in the room.

We keep doing it places we are more likely to get caught cause its more exciting. We sometimes forget ourselves in our family room and we'll start mindlessly caressing each other while watching TV or something. I think my mom suspects something but I'm not sure.

505976245

Masturbating to Internet porn (I'm a girl) with one hand and eating Cheetos with the other, I suddenly realized there was no way I could save the mouse...never have I felt so pathetic.

<u>820715828</u>

Me and my cousin...both guys...we used to fuck around when we were kids. Like 6-8, somewhere around then. Just get naked with each other in the dark fool around. We'd bargain with sexual favours, each act having its own value for an amount of time. Heh.

Anyway, then he moved away and I saw him last year with the whole family get together. We're both in college and I'm a pretty weird kid, he is totally like Mr. Jock-frat-boy etc. I wonder if he remembers that shit, cuz I sure didn't for a long time. Heh.

What sucks is that now I am sooooo totally comfortable with touching guys, even though I'm not attracted to them. But girls still have this like...mystique I haven't broken yet, just as far as like touching on the casual level ya know. Damn.

<u>120137437</u>

When I was in high school, there was a girl in my jour-nalism class a couple years younger than me who was completely in love with me. She would talk to me on the Internet and flirt like mad, and sometimes I would do it back just for the thrill.

One night while I was with some friends, she called me very drunk and started asking me why I wouldn't fall in love with her. I was confused and asked her to elaborate. She told me if I came over, we could do things with no strings attached.

So I told my friends I was going to McDonald's, got in my car, sped over to her house, picked her up, fucked her without a condom in the backseat and came on her face. When we were done I felt really dirty and told her this was the first and last time. I took her home and was back at my friend's house within 45 minutes.

I said the drive-thru guys fucked up my McFlurry.

She sent me an e-mail the next day sounding scared and asking if it was a dream. I never replied. I feel like such an ass.

At the same time though, I feel like such a fuckin' porn star. Consequently, I'm going to hell.

574161640

When I was in 8th grade, I visited my father for the summer break. He works for the government and couldn't get off of work for a week. My stepmother worked 3 days a week, taking care of retards in the city (40 minute drive).

I was alone for 3 days in my dad's house . . . 800 miles from my own. Most of the time, I just watched satellite TV or looked at his *Playboy* or *Hustler* magazines. Sometimes, I would go on explorations of the house, snooping through shit that wasn't mine to see what all I could find.

In the bathroom, I found my stepmothers dildo. I wondered why she would have this, her and my dad have plenty of sex together. None the less, I licked it. She's not an attractive woman, I just couldn't resist. I did this for a couple of seconds and then I realized a dildo is an imitation of a penis, and this might be gay. I dropped it, it was made out of plastic and the plastic cracked. Batteries fell out.

I then put it back together the best that I could and hid it where the found it. The next day I asked my dad if he and

I could go to Walmart and get a model. On the second day they left, I used the superglue from the model on the dildo. It was as good as new.

Before I left I stole about 25 issues of *Hustler, Penthouse,* and *Playboy,* I put them in my backpack and prayed to god it wouldn't be searched at the airport. I still have 3 of these magazines. When I got back, I had sold them for 5-25 dollars to friends.

The following summer I started hanging out with more chicks. I got a lot of oral sex and had actual sex with 1 girl about 10 times. My mom would frequently piss away our money on useless shit. We have over $6,000 in DVDs. Our phone got turned off and there was a bill for $120 dollars. She went into my room one day looking for money to "borrow" and found my condoms. When she saw this, she took my money, paid the phone bill, and didn't mention anything to me for about a week.

A week later she confronted me with a box of condoms and told me she was sad to see that I was having sex, being only 15 at the time. She was, of course, crying. I didn't know what to say so I just let her do most of the talking. She then told me she tried to find a positive outlook on the whole subject and it was that at least I was using condoms. She told me she had herpes. I was appalled by this. She said she had got it from my father who got it from my stepmother while he was cheating on my mother.

I remembered the dildo incident and became sick to my stomach. Luckily I have never had a cold sore 4 years after the incident. I hope that I didn't contract anything... and I hope that neither my dad or stepmom ever come to this site because I'm sure if they came acrossed this they would be able to put 2 and 2 together.

Typing all of that brought back a feeling of fear. Remembering how it all was, but I haven't told one soul until now. It feels better to get it out, I suppose.

314250330

I had a dream about some girl wanting me to eat cat food from her puss. I wonder what **that** means...

840305094

One day, I walked into my friend's dorm room to microwave my cup of noodles. She was having sex with her boyfriend, but I didn't care. I microwaved my noodles anyway. And then I offered her some. Her boyfriend was about to cum, but I didn't care, I was hungry.

640150290

I've looked at so much Internet porn that when I see an MPEG or AVI icon I get turned on.

591181852

Sometimes when I masturbate, my father pops into my head. I am totally grossed out and have to stop. I wish this wouldn't happen.

890719026

Last Christmas my stepsister and I came back from college to visit the family. Christmas Eve night while putting things in our parents and little siblings stockings, she asked me if I wanted to smoke pot. We ended up having intercourse and feeling very awkward around each other on Christmas. The part I am most weirded out about is we did it again the night after too.

I find that I am completely obsessed with underage girls lately. My coworker's daughter is 13 and comes by most days after school. She hangs about, quietly, reading or doing homework, sometimes talking to us, and I find her absolutely attractive. It is to the point that I would die just to be with her. I watch her furtively when she's here, looking at her small frame, pretty eyes and mouth, and the way she dresses. Today was the first day she's come by for a week or two (she was out of school) and I realize that I just don't get any work done for the last couple hours of my day when she's there. Eventually I have to slink away to the toilet and masturbate.

Worse, this is part of a pattern in my life that has simply escalated. I just don't find mature women attractive anymore. When I look at a crowd, my eye is drawn by the abundance of Lolitas...I look for their big eyes and freckly skin and small chests and tiny waists and buttocks, and love the way they dress, showing off so much hip and belly when they can, their tiny perfect toes in sandals when the weather is warm, their precocious makeup and sometimes piercings. I don't find pre-pubescent girls attractive, the objects of my attentions are always sexually ripe, like from 12 or 13 onwards. But beyond a certain age, she could stride by in the nude, and I wouldn't glance twice. My girlfriend is 4 years younger than me (I'm 28) and she's beautiful and slim but when we have sex it's difficult for me. I like to imagine she's half her age, but I know I'm fooling myself, and I'll drop her eventually. And eventually...I feel like eventually I'll be arrested for contributing to the delinquency of a minor or something, I don't know. But there's no legal release for my affections. I wish there were.

169821305

I'm jacking off as you read this.

374803314

I secretly wish that men I knew masturbated while thinking of me.

358132043

I want to do my manager in the worst way...He has a girlfriend but he flirts with me all the time. I really just want
him to throw me down on the counter or in the storage
room and have his way with me. I think he knows I want
him. But I can't outright tell him. 'Cause that's sexual
harassment or something. I don't think he would care. I
want his sex so bad.

Also, I have an addiction to pistachios.

396938617

The first time I ever masturbated was in the shower on a
Sunday morning. The second time was in the church
bathroom about an hour later.

17567544

I have had sex on a large airplane at cruising altitude.

4750216

I like feet more than the average person.

844511034

When I'm feeling especially depressed, I masturbate up

to 5 times a day. I've done it on several occasions in airplane bathrooms, in hotel rooms with sleeping people present and once in the backseat of a car that my parents were driving at the time.

On the same note, I regularly think about girls I'm friends with and it makes me feel like I'm violating them, but I'm too weak to stop.

101765867

Today is pajama day in the office and I have no underwear on.

121285088

I'm 17 and I still use the small spoons.

369480504

I really enjoy squeezing out ingrown hairs... This is the main reason I get my bikini line waxed, for some reason I always get more there.

241677804

I sniff my dad's underwear. I'm a guy.

284137129

I always wanted to try it on with my best girl mate... I'm a little curious! Well one night, I finally managed to b in a situation with her that she was willing to experiment with a girl too...namely me! Well, we went to my place, started touchy-feely, when suddenly my older brother opens my bedroom door to c me down on her! Not a good sight!

653205288

I dated this boy for about four months last year and I really hated him, but the first month or so that we were together, he went down on me and it was so, so good, and the only reason I stayed with him was because he was good at everything sexual. He just sucked at life, and I still hate him, and he still talks to me occasionally, and the only reason I actually talk back is the fact that I am infatuated with his best friend.

875288457

I once masturbated while working at the parish rectory. I was 13 and bored, and the priests were all asleep. I think that bought my ticket into hell.

116131929

I kissed my first cousin and almost had sex with him even though I was 17 and he was 26. It went on for quite a while. I had a boyfriend at the time.

118977423

I'm 17 female and I took a 25 yr old male's virginity and that was my oldest virgin.

490237420

When I was in 6th grade, I went down on my best friend and she went down on me...we did it all the time...now we never speak.

692883827

I'm totally in love with this guy in my gym class...I look at his year book picture every night and kiss it, then lay in bed fantasizing about him kissing me... God I need a life...

918139842

I like to wear fishnet stockings under my pants. It makes me feel more confident. I'm a 4th grade male school-teacher and if anyone ever found out I'm sure they would fire me.

675222773

I sometimes wish that I could be a wolf or a dog just so I could be able to lick my partner's genitals in public without being arrested...I'm gay, but I'd go bi if I could do that.

I also worry that this desire to be like a dog could lead to bestiality like Jeffrey Dahmer's repressed homosexuality supposedly led him to murder and rape little boys. I don't want to fuck dogs. I want to be one.

911849328

I want to sleep with my brother.

533697345

I want to build a man that I can have gay sex with, a mixture of all the guys I have ever wanted.

299159240

As a younger man, I would often find myself stealing glances at the genitalia of passing dogs. Afterwards I would often be so racked with guilt I would flay myself with an unraveled wire coat hanger.

415590019

Sometimes when I'm shaving, I will purposely not shave between my upper lip and nose. This leaves a good amount of shaving cream on that part of my face, which forms a Hitler-esque mustache... and then I walk around my dorm room naked, yelling "**seig heil!**"

420971648

I've just had the strangest, dirtiest fantasy:

My girlfriend goes down on me, gets really into it and eyes closed in ecstasy, slowly bites clean through the base of my penis, before swallowing it and smiling.

It just popped into my head but now it's turning me on. I really want her to bite me.

354802535

I faked sick and stayed home from school on 11/22/63, I was in my room poundin' my pud when my mother rushed in and told me Kennedy was shot...I feel like it's all my fault.

937205178

I'm a 79-year-old grandmother of two, I regularly sit near to people on the bus who I find attractive and purr at them.

This does include females.

423006690

I had sex with Dustin Diamond (Screech from "Saved by the Bell") — no joke.

865732533

My life is over. Three days ago I awoke from a sexy dream to find myself having sex with my brothers feet. He was awake and he just said go back to bed. I know he's going to tell dad.

585546211

I like to masturbate while driving, its like killing 2 birds with one stone.

252947021

Today I was walking to my friend's house and I dropped my lollipop in the dirt. I picked it up, licked it, spit out the dirt, and continued on my way.
I'm dirty.

127709109

I like to go down on my wife while she talks on the phone with her parents. I whisper the childhood nickname her father gave her while I do it.

353546778

I kissed ten people in one night.

Seven of them were girls.

I'm female and straight as a ruler.

786078571

Nearly every night I sneak out of our Amish community to read grouphug in the library.

556596680

I get horny while watching girls brush their teeth, especially when they are in their pajamas. It makes me want to "badger the witness."

451607861

I enjoy pissing down children's playground equipment during the night. It's just liberating.

438682702

I found a porno under my mom and dad's bed. I jerk off a lot. So I thought this may be nice. When I found the tape I realized I was watching my dad having sex with a prostitute. I kept watching. My dad has a small penis.

141006758

When I found out that my car key could unlock my mate's car, I went there one night, unlocked it and shat all over the driver's seat before locking it and sneaking off. A week later, I sent him an anonymous "ransom note" style letter, stating that "his time was nigh," signed the "phantom crapper."

445200705

You know what's fun? Making waffles naked, leggo my eggo.

394059050

I have a fantasy about spanking this woman I know. I ask her for a $1. She hands me a bill, and I crack her on the ass the number of times as the last two digits of the serial number on the bill. I prop her butt up on some pillows and use a belt.

108356332

I wipe standing up. I am the only person I know who does this.

930378882

Someone at work stuck a giant penis to my terminal to surprise me. However, I'm having the last laugh as I'm taking it home for my own use.

178205418

When I was a kid, I thought I was the reincarnation of Jesus. Every once in awhile, I still do.

904200996

One time when my girlfriend was having an orgasm on the phone with me, I recorded it and I put it on my computer and burned it onto CD and I sent it to all my Internet friends. And I jerk off to it, and I gave copies of it that I burnt onto CD to random kids that trick-or-treated at my house on Halloween. I labeled those CD's "Avril Lavigne featuring Eminem" but it was actually just a few minutes of my girlfriend having an orgasm.

868557309

All the times I've ever had sex in my life were for the purpose of burning calories, whether I liked the person or not.

239023241

I jerk off in church.

638125514

I allowed my boyfriend to pee on me. It's a huge fetish for him. He begged me for days and I said no for a while but then finally gave in under the condition that it could only happen in the shower. Well it's 3 days later and about 6 showers later and I still feel dirty. I'm really fearful he's going to want to do more. It grosses me out so much! Eww!

146922784

When I was a little girl, 7 or 8 years old, I would go with my mother (who was a caregiver for the mentally challenged) to work. One time I was alone with one of her patients (he was 30something) and...I touched his wee-wee.

344486277

I masturbated with a cucumber. I washed it and a few days later my mom used it in a salad.

591875629

I have a recurring fantasy about being a man and being seduced by a male psychiatrist while playing the piano. I'm a female.

217420970

I had sex in a cemetery last weekend. Up against a tombstone. I'm going to hell for sure.

327885315

I wish I had a stalker who was obsessed with me. That would totally turn me on.

494275209

I think I'm into bestiality.

395210322

When I was babysitting in middle school & high school, I used to look through the kids parents' video collections looking for porn. I'd dig way in the back & everything. Found some once. :)

345983654

I have masturbated at work and then not washed my hands and gone back to my desk.

397804084

I want to touch boobs more than I want to touch my boyfriend's penis.

465912961

Sometimes I'd rather masturbate, than have sex with my wife.

She's just sooooo boring in bed.

996695837

I worry that I'm boring in bed.

910116713

Any time I ever have a one-night stand, I apologize afterwards and say, "I don't usually do this." I think they're lying, too.

648507515

A year later and I still fall asleep thinking about last year's summer fling.

194622194

I love to masturbate. I mean I really love to masturbate. I think about ways to go home during the workday to rub one out. If I could spend just 2 days off during the week, I would rent 3 new DVDs and make love to myself so much I would feel the need to cheat on myself with my girlfriend just to break the habit.

322419855

Reading all of these confessions makes me feel better, but it also makes me want to meet some of the girls who are confessing because they seem like they'd be fun to mess around with.

279686639

I fantasize about dudes who wear gold chains, walkmans, baggy pants and coogi sweaters on the subway and sway their heads to the music. I want to rip their clothes off, unless they have bad acne.

770952236

I've had sex w/hookers...multiple times...while my wife...and my boss, watched.

486982915

I just had my first homosexual experience.

245481294

I think the girl I slept with last night stole my left shoe. I wish I had asked her what her name was.

392921459

I remember being about three or four years old when I walked past a shut bedroom door and peeped through the old-fashioned keyhole; I have a vague recollection of seeing my parents in their underclothes sort of touching each other.

I liked wearing my sister's dresses and pretending I was a girl. The fancy stopped when I walked out the front door and our neighbour, who was standing across the fence, saw me and laughed. I was about 10. Another time, our babysitter, who was a 17 year-old boy (who I had a mild crush on), tried fondling me when I was in one of those dresses. I screamed and he stopped.

I stole an ornament from one of my teachers when I was 11.

I used to fantasize about my music teacher in primary school. He was very muscle-y and the kids used to laugh about him being macho and fondling the girls. I wanted to be fondled!

I used to pick my nose and leave the "findings" under furniture. (Thank goodness I've become a clean freak and stopped that now!)

When I was 12, I was holding a puppy on my lap, and he started licking my crotch. I couldn't cum yet, but the buzz in my genitals was electrifying, and I just let him.

When I first started I could only masturbate with both hands. And I was paranoid about not getting my cum anywhere but into a tissue.

In my teens, male underwear really turned me on. Occasionally, when I went over to people's places, I'd steal my friend's or father's underwear, take it home, sniff it, wear it, and masturbate.

Oddest places I've masturbated:

> a. In my classroom in Year 10 — came in my pants and stayed the rest of the school day without cleaning myself. It was such a turn on!

> b. Behind a bush close to home. It was pretty late coming home from a party, and I was so horny. I kind of liked the idea of playing with myself in public and the risk of getting caught.

I left a window open, and one of our (indoor) cats jumped out and got mauled and killed by a pack of dogs. I cried heaps, because I was closest to her, but I didn't have the guts to admit to my family that it was my fault.

I cheated on my boyfriend when he had gone interstate to study for six months. I had five or six (safe) one-night stands during that time. I broke up with him when he returned, but didn't confess my infidelity. Oddly, our sex got amazingly better after the break-up. Two years on, we're best friends now and don't have sex, but I'm still afraid to tell him about my cheating days out of shame and for fear of hurting him.

In spite of all of this, I'm happy, healthy, sane and successful. I accept my past as experiences necessary for my development. Moderators, thanks for the opportunity to vent.

825550166

I'm a bloke who has read a lot of feminist criticism/gender studies etc. over the years. I saw *The Hours* and thought it rocked. Virginia Woolf, Edith Wharton — I love 'em. Nonetheless, I like hookers. No two ways around it. Only been with 4 in like the last 10 years, but if I was wealthy, could get it away with it, and not get diseases, I would do it all the time. I'm happily married, and haven't done it since then, but if given the chance I doubt if I'd be able to control myself. I screwed one in a foreign country once — she had enormous, sculpted fake tits, was probably all of 16, even had braces (her pimps surely paid for her accessories). Another time I got a BJ in a car in the inner city, and I think it was a man. Was one tall chick in any event. I'm afraid if I ever went to Thailand, with the boys, or on my own, I'd never come back. I start working some shit job and just live like a lustful rabbit. How sick!

143980341

One time, my sister's boyfriend was sleeping in the bunk above me and I couldn't sleep, so when everyone had gone to bed and he was asleep, I copped a feel. That is, I dug a tunnel through his covers and reached into his boxers.

I am ashamed of this because I am a guy.

I do not want to be gay.

Gay is not accepted.

920206877

I was feeling a little "lonely" last night. I thought I would feel better if I put the vacuum cleaner hose on my penis. I did feel better last night, but my girlfriend came home and saw me. She started crying. She just doesn't understand about the vacuum thing. Now I feel guilty about it.

For years I either allowed people to assume — or intimated that — I had a college degree of some sort. I may have even (foolhardily and likely very drunk) dropped a name of a school or two. It got to a point where I was resenting people for even asking. I didn't want it to matter, and lying in mixed company can require excruciating explanations, lies to cover for lies, and awesome diplomatic finesse.

I stopped the insinuation a while back but haven't exactly come clean about it. The ugly truth is that I dropped out of college to get a piece of the dot com money.

685625738

My mate is going out with a girl I picked up in a bar and took home for a night over a year ago. Me and the girl have talked about it but we still haven't told him.

818932705

When I was 12, I met this older boy at the mall. He thought I was a girl and I didn't tell him otherwise. We snuck off into an employee's only area behind the food court and I performed oral sex on him. He wanted to do the same to me but I was afraid he'd beat me up if he found out I was a boy.

I wasn't even dressed like a girl or anything. I was just

wearing a t-shirt and cut-offs. I looked very girlish though (still do).

I feel guilty for not letting him know before I did it that I was a boy. I feel like I used him. It was one of the best sexual experiences of my life though and if I had it to do all over again I would.

He probably bragged to all his friends about the hot little girl that blew him at the mall.

I never saw him again.

I wonder if he still thinks of me.

342422635

The only girlfriend I have ever had is one that I met online. She gave me a **fake** pic. Didn't tell me it was fake until months later. I forgave her at the time being that I knew I had no one else...its been more than a year now and I really want to break it off. We have met once and it wasn't too great. She showed me a pic of her friend which is the total opposite of everything she is. I regret giving her a chance when she told me that she was really not the person in the pic she had first given me.

386919418

I buy CDs that I think will look impressive in my collection. I want to give the impression that I am "musically educated." I'm such a tool.

637330429

I did an evil thing. In September of 2002 I got drunk and slept with this girl I would have never hooked up with had I been sober. A few months later around April of

2003 I get a call from her and she tells me that she is pregnant. At first I got real worried but then I realized it was only once, I used protection and this girl really gets around. I consoled her and told her I would be there to help in any way I could. At the time I was bs-ing her but then an evil plot hatched in my mind. My favorite band Phish was set to start touring in July (now it was late May) and I had tickets to see a few shows. I really wanted to go on a whole tour like I used to do in college but now I had a real job making such getaways tough. I work for a large corporation with great benefits. I saw my way to exploit the system. The company I work for gives an extra week of vacation time and $500 to newlyweds and two weeks vacation and check of $1000 to parents of newborns. I realized if I married this girl and admitted to being the father of this child I could possibly get enough time off work to go on tour and a nice check to help finance it. By the first week of June we were at the courthouse for a shotgun wedding, the baby was born on June 15th and by July 1st I had three extra weeks of unused vacation time and a check for $500 and $1000. The Phish tour started on July 7th, by the 5th I was on the road to Phoenix. I up and left her without saying a word and did not return home until August 5th two days after the tour ended. Needless to say she was an emotional wreck. I however had one more ace up my sleeve...I demanded a paternity test pronto. Sure enough the test came back clearing me of my obligation to her and the child and I had seen most every show on the tour! I felt bad for a while but she should have never rushed into marriage without knowing who the real father was and I was able to have the divorce complete by the time I went to Miami this past December for Phish's New Year's run.

661333789

I sent an e-mail to a wonderful young man, a very smart

teacher's assistant at a respected college. It was the begin-ning of the school year, and I had to tell him how much I loathed and hated his facial hair. It sounds silly, I know, but he's a very handsome and talented man that looked like a child molester with that awful mustache. In my stupid logic I thought it would help him if I told him to get rid of it. It might one day cost him a job or a girlfriend. An old teacher of mine once said that his wife had found a picture of him that was taken three weeks before they first met. A picture in which he had a big stupid mus-tache and she said right there that she would have never given him a chance if he had that facial hair when they met. Time passed. I got an angry response via e-mail from the teacher's assistant. I felt bad about it, but stopped thinking about it shortly after. Later I found out that he got his brother involved, the two of them researched to find the identity of the fake name I supplied and deduced that it was from his cousin that works nearby. There had been some bad noise between them before, and when he confronted her about the mustache e-mail she denied it and turned red, which incriminated her all the more. He said he was going to take pictures of the cousin's work building and send them to her signed with the fake name I had used. I never meant to cause him or his family all of this discomfort. I feel terrible about it, and I know he will never find out it is me unless I one day crack and tell him. If anyone has ever read *Crime and Punishment*, I feel like I am sitting, squirming in front of the detective Porfiry Petrovich when ever I see him.

741813578

I sent in a confession a while ago, and now I have an up-date. It was about a mean e-mail I sent to a very nice teacher's assistant at a respectable art school. In the e-mail I told him that his mustache was horrible and would probably cost him future success. I did this for his sake because in high school I had a teacher who said that his wife found an old picture of him taken when he had a mustache and she said that she would have never given him a chance if he had that awful facial hair when they met.

I had forgotten about the nasty e-mail I sent to the T.A., but discovered that he had not and he and his brother had been researching and trying to figure out who had sent it. They wrongly assumed that it was their cousin, and when they confronted her about it she got red-faced and flustered, which they believed incriminated her all the more. He's taken to stalking her and taking pictures of her at work and mailing them to her and signing them with the fake name I used. I felt really awful about it, but the other day I saw him, and he shaved the mustache off and looks ten times better. Way to go handsome T.A.!

870102758

My parents abused me, both physically an emotionally. I never really thought it was a big deal because it wasn't as much as some kids (well, at least not the physical abuse) so I never told anyone.

One time I went to school with a black eye, and I guess a teacher reported it to child protection, and they came to my house to investigate. My parents were really mad at me and thought that I either called child protection or told a teacher to call them. They told me I was going to be responsible for breaking up the family and I would have to go live in an orphanage. So I lied about what happened and said that my parents never hit me.

485812290

I cheated my way through college using Cliff notes and copying off of other people's tests.

I did more work finding random books to copy my master's thesis than probably would have taken to just do the thesis myself.

My resume is total bull shit, except for the fact that I do have a master's degree (which was described above), and I use friends who lie for me as references and make me look better than I am.

I am seriously under-qualified for the position I have at work.

There are people with higher education than me, work harder than me, who make tens of thousands of dollars less than I do at this company.

I can't say I really feel that bad about all of this, because I'm a really good "people person." I've bull-shitted my way through the majority of my life, and I'm a very successful business person — at least everyone else thinks so.

I have an office full of books I've only skimmed enough though to be able to talk about them for a short time.

I take the maximum allowable charitable donation for church on my taxes, but I do not donate because I know it's something that doesn't raise a "red flag" with the IRS.

I feel like no one even knows me, but it's too late to do anything about it.

I will probably marry my long time girlfriend and have children and raise them to be upstanding citizens - "because look how far that got daddy."

Life is what you make of it I guess.

I often wonder what it is like to be real.

<u>105213203</u>

I've always joined a church in whatever community I've moved into in order to gain an entrance into the community, and it's worked for me most of the time, but I have never experienced God the way my fellow Christians claim that they do. Intellectually I believe in a creator and intelligent design, because it seems more logical than believing that the universe is an accident, but I have never felt the warm personal connection to Him that one is supposed to. I pray, but I feel silly doing so, like I'm pretending or just talking to myself. There is Asperger's in the family; my son was diagnosed, and I feel I probably have it too although I was not diagnosed, maybe this prevents me from experiencing God the way others do.

I can't help feeling that religion is a method by which people acquire ascendancy over other people. I don't believe in the inerrancy of the Bible. It was written by a bunch of Middle Eastern men, with the kind of agendas that you would expect Middle Eastern men to have. I was married to a Middle Eastern man once. It didn't work out. I would love to know, love and adore God the way I've always heard you're supposed to, but I am working on a novel and I don't expect the characters I have created to know, love and adore me.

My life seems to have been like a California peach — it's gone from hard and unripe to dry and mushy without any period of juicy deliciousness in between. That's why I hope that there's reincarnation. Maybe next time will be better.

<u>256494141</u>

I forged a "free pie" coupon at Marie Callender's, and gave it to my wife. I didn't tell her it was a forged coupon, and she got arrested.

Bail is $750, and I can't afford it, so she's still in County Jail.

Sorry, honey!

713021437

I am the biggest hypocrite. I am a woman of 18 with an extremely trendy-but-conventional group of friends, and I pretend to be a lesbian in order to seem... what? Daring? Distinguished? Different?

I swan around flamboyantly with my hands on my hips pointing out at 300 decibels the girls I supposedly "like." Her. And her. **And** her. In fact...every girl in this whole damn room.

I always drop the subject in conversation. "What's your opinion on the Iraq war?" "Well as a lesbian I feel..."

I get annoyed at men who try it on with me. So you want to go out with me, **boy**? How dare you? Don't you know I'm a fucking dyke? Isn't it apparent in my every move?

The truth? My straightness would not disgrace a spirit level.

...I am not proud.

634693507

I made some marijuana brownies one day, and when I left them to cool my mother came home from work and ate almost half of them. She had never been stoned before, and when she got the massive hit she curled up in a ball on the ground in her room, screaming that she was dying. She made me write her a new will, in which the goldfish would inherit the house. I never told her that it was brownies that made her so sick, and she's still convinced it was a bad oyster she had for lunch.

542899494

At college I grab girls rear-ends and say, "Hey Jessica."

Then apologize and say they looked really like my best girl friend from behind — And get away with it all the time.

690776059

I am only attracted to white guys, even though men of every race, color, and creed come on to me.

I'm so racist that I've only been on dates with two guys who had brown eyes. And they had the kind of brown eyes where you could actually see separate irises and pupils. I once rejected a really nice guy because his eyes were entirely black, so black they seemed extra liquidy. He was just not white enough.

I sometimes manage to skirt the issue by telling my friends I'm really into blond guys when they want to set me up on blind dates.

I'm secretly jealous of Jewish people who only want to date other Jews because they almost never have to justify only dating other white people. I know there are some adopted Jews and converts of other races, but it's a miniscule number compared to the overall whiteness of that faith.

I also sometimes skirt the issue by saying my dad will kill me if I don't marry someone Irish or Irish-American, when he has in fact never said anything of the kind.

46248294

I lied to my prom date about being grounded so I wouldn't have to take him along on the trip to the lake after prom. He found out when we got back to school. Then I picked up our prom pictures and never gave him any. I still feel horrible about it.

866437997

I am a homosexual film star, but my wife doesn't even know. I have been in the business for 13 years.

376174134

I go to school with a blind girl. I made friends with her, but now I kinda regret it. She's always asking me to walk her to class, always calling me, and always asking me to take her everywhere. It's kind of an inconvenience for me but I always feel bad when I tell her I can't. But inside I just wanna yell "Don't you have any other friends? I don't wanna be your personal assistant, damn it! Fuck Off!" What makes it worse is that she doesn't wanna help herself. She likes being completely dependent on others and it pisses me off! Somebody asked her once if she would ever consider getting a dog to guide her and she said **no** really fast. I feel really bad for thinking like this but, that quickly subsides...

777423843

I deduced that my girlfriend reads my journal, but I read her e-mails and she doesn't know. Dare I cuss her out for violating my privacy?

338811690

I was on a sex "sabbatical" and told all my friends about it, the purpose being that I needed to focus on my goals and not be distracted by boys, because I tend to meet a lot of them. Well...long story short, the sabbatical ended this weekend...after only 7 weeks. God I'm so weak. However, it was a bloody good time with this bloke and his man member was huge...so I don't regret it. I just regret telling all my friends that I was going to "rise above my desires" and then I lost control.

361600376

I check out fat ugly men so they don't feel so ugly...

883431069

I once stole a car, broke all the windows, and left it in a parking garage. I gave the man I stole the car from a description of the person who I said was trying to open his vehicle. He called the police and they arrested the person I had described. This other person was my uncle who had just been released from prison and was on 10 month probation for grand theft auto. I don't know why I did this, I regret it, and no one knows.

My uncle is still in jail.

553528919

In 5th grade this kid I didn't like had broken his foot. I told him I was going to step on it and he said I wouldn't. I stomped on it as hard as I could. He was so delirious from the pain that he told the principal it was the kid on the other side of him in line. The other kid was suspended.

875021364

I gave a sympathy fuck this summer to a guy whose girlfriend died suddenly. He was so sad, so desperate... and so freakin' drunk! But we had been lovers for a while, and it was comfort for him, I guess.

He clung to me while we were screwing, like I was going to just slip away.

I feel bad because he was all "I love you, I love you," while we were doing it, and I said it back, but I was no longer in love with him.

Sorry, babe.

694852420

I had my 13 year-old dog put to sleep because it was really starting to bug me but I convinced my wife and the vet that it was sick.

652914305

I vacuumed over my baby brother's foot and it sucked all his skin off the top of his foot.

He couldn't talk, only cry. He screamed and howled bloody murder. I ran off.

I never let on that I knew anything about it and pretended it must have been an accident.

550864131

I played solitaire while my gf masturbated over the phone. I'm not secretly gay or anything, I had just finished already. And I won the game. :D

171068386

I messed around with my brother's CD player then

thought I broke it. I threw it in the woods, and he thought he lost it. Mom got mad at him and I let him take it the whole time. I also used peanut butter with my dog.

814619869

One time my little brother was pestering the hell out of me and he would not cease, so I bit my arm as hard as I could and blamed the teeth-marks on him. He sat in the corner for the rest of the night while I played with his He-Man action figures.

342249937

I hid a magnetic strip thing deep inside my dad's wallet after he pissed me off one day. He gets stopped at every store for setting off the alarm and can't figure out why. It's been 9 months of this. I'm starting to feel bad about it...

942178906

In kindergarten, this girl Vicki lost a baby tooth in class. She put it in her cubby. I stole it from her cubby to put under my pillow. I remember how much she cried when she realized it was gone. I didn't tell my parents since I thought they would be able to see it wasn't mine. I put it under my pillow, but the tooth fairy never came to bring me my 25 cents. Hence, I've had the tooth ever since reminding me every day of what I did. Sorry Vicki. Please forgive me.

393778192

I get girls in the sack by acting like a righteous homosexual who's "saving himself." When they "find out" that it's them I want to "lose it with," they totally fall for it. I then resume acting gay, and ask them not to say anything. They never do.

413857026

I want to be the better person after this break up, but only so I can rub her face in it.

912401283

I lie all the time. I lie to myself that I lie.

170172015

At the time I got pregnant, I was sleeping with 3 or 4 guys. I told the one that I thought it was that he was definitely the father...but there's still some doubt in my mind.

132686982

I shot myself in the foot, just to get sympathy from my unloving boyfriend, friends, and family. In fact, I made a couple new friends from this God awful experience. Then, to keep the whole thing going I told everyone that the reason I was shot in the foot is because I was robbed and I wrestled the guy to the ground. I also told them that I could have a bad case of gangrene. They believe every word I say...and I don't feel any bit of remorse.

432563812

This boy fell asleep in my art class yesterday so my friends and I put crayons up his nose.

He was pretty mad when he woke up so I apologized and even made him an "I'm sorry I put crayons in your nose while you were sleeping" tape.

The truth is, I'm not really that sorry, and I'd definitely do it again.

410027857

On New Year's Eve of Y2K, I was really nervous after buying condoms and beer with a fake ID that I backed out of the parking lot into the driver's side door of a really fucking nice Lexus.

I was so shocked that I just froze in the place until some kids (15 or 16) started yelling, "Just go, dude! Just go!!! **Get outta here! Quick!!**"

So I did and I've been paranoid ever since.

273125796

Once when I was in high school, I hurled a piece of poop at the mirrors in the bathroom. I was valedictorian, but that was the most worthwhile thing I ever did in that awful place

928895566

I one time hit a person in a crosswalk with my car late at night. Rather than stop and make sure they were ok, I sped off. That night I tore the license plates off my car and the next day reported them stolen to the cops.

671965799

I deleted a voicemail to my boyfriend from his ex. She wanted him to pick her up from the airport. Needless to say, no one picked her up. And I don't feel bad about it.

833815399

I was backing my car out turned it too quick and rubbed up against my dad's new truck. No damage to his, but my car broke the front headlight out and left a scratch.

I prayed for a week that he wouldn't see it then some guy hit me, totaled my car, and daddy never knew what happened to my headlight.

Yay!

533194744

I was once fooling around with a guy I hardly knew, lost interest and feigned sleep so he would leave.

545004748

I tell my wife I'm glad I got out of the Marine Corps so I can be with her.

I should never have gotten out of the Marine Corps.

849411992

I had gay sex when I was younger, and the only reason I don't still do it is because I'm too much of a pussy now and I'm concerned about what everyone else will think.

748853916

In high school, I drove a pretty cool car for a sixteen year old. One day, a known "bad girl" asked to borrow my car for a few hours. I allowed her to, as I was desperate to be liked by all in my school. I was supposed to leave school early that day, and I told her to have my car back by 11 AM. When I went to leave school at that time, she had yet to return my car to its parking spot. I then went to the office, and told the administration that she had actually stolen the keys out of my locker, and in turn had stolen my car. The police were called, and a search began. Eventually, the car was found at her house. I pressed charges, cried to the police when they suggested that I had given her my car (which was obviously the story she had given them, as it was the truth). The police believed me, as my parents were known throughout the community, and she was sent to a juvenile center for her last year of high school. She was forced to pay restitution as well, since I said I had approximately $100 bucks that was stolen from my glove compartment. She had to also write me an apology. Her life was ruined, but I had told her to have the car back by a certain time. Taught her to mess with me....

➤

It's possible that I met Leah in September. Rather, I didn't meet her but was alerted to her by my alert friend Daniel. Daniel was at home with his records and vintage Playboy but it seemed to be our mutual concern with one particular woman that we had most in common. Daniel was interested in indie-pop. He was indie-hip. We were walking to Frank and Angie's pizzeria one Wednesday when he offhandedly noted "Leah has a boyfriend. She's been with him for six years." My interest was casual at the time but this was a disappointing blow nonetheless. It would be weeks before I would meet Leah's boyfriend, but I would know a few things about him by the time I met him.

I had an Eames chair near my desk at the ridiculous startup where Leah and I met. I didn't own it and I never sat in it. We acquired all of our office furniture from a second-hand business furniture warehouse and separated our work areas via shoji screens and strands of beads. My desk was no more than ten yards from hers but we didn't speak until she asked me where I got the chair. In the course of a dozen emails back and forth she asked what I did, what kind of music I like, and could she perhaps have the chair? My answers were uninteresting or unsatisfactory enough for her to bring up her boyfriend. She wondered if I might be able to get him a job. Fuck!

After a few days of casual and infrequent banter, we had lunch together at Frank and Angie's. We sat at a small table against a wall, she west of me. Her face starts with a nice chin, is prone to blushing, and was framed by a chunky black bob, tucked behind her ears *in anticipation of our mediocre lunch. I don't remember what I ordered — I probably didn't eat it. Leah kicked off the conversation by asking if I liked being single. She came to confess that she had been, for some time, on the verge of breaking up with her boyfriend. Allow me pause to point out this classic manipulation: committed individual hints to potential new catch that he or she may be imminently loosed from bondage; potential new catch sees, of course, a glimmer of hope in this and immediately ceases all other pursuits. It's a nasty business but it works. I was damn near smitten. Dutifully I labored on about the benefits of single life, blah blah blah. (The truth is that I absolutely hate being single. I hate dating and, even more, I hate not knowing when I'm going to get some hot making-out-with-the-cute-new-girl romancing.) We both knew that we were fully engaged in a game now. She acted like she wanted to be single and I acted like there was nothing in the world as fantastic and exciting as being lonely. It was all a sham and in a thousand years, when the species is more enlightened, we'll skip the charade and make love right at Frank and Angie's.*

I'm certain there were other lunches, other in-office opportunities to talk about why I was better than what's-his-name, but the next outing that comes to mind is a show at La Zona Rosa. We showed up separately, meeting a bunch of people from work, probably coordinated by Daniel. Leah arrived in beautiful form. Her hair was jet black (Clairol Blue-Black, actually), tucked behind her ears, and as shiny as her painted, lined, glossed lips. She was wearing a dangerously tight vinyl jacket (also remarkably shiny) with almost-as-tight Levis and finally, the compulsory black Camper shoes. Rehanging her black Manhattan Portage bag on her shoulder, she bounced up, said something funny and glib about the venue, and announced that the other guy was staying in tonight. Outstanding!

Several gin and tonics later Leah and I were an inseparable, giggling pair of fourth-graders: one of those touchy, happy couples that I can't stand to look at. I ignored warning glances from a couple of friend girls, who absolutely revel in giving warning glances.

I know of two ways to make a horny guy try to kiss a pretty girl. First, you can tell him to kiss you. Second, you can tell him not to. Leah emailed me at work the next morning:

Hey Gabriel,

Daniel pulled me aside this morning and told me that we're "ruining the group dynamic."

Promise me we won't do anything stupid like sleeping together.

Leah

I knew what it means. But no, she was right: that would be bad. I'm not that kind of person. Six years, she'd been with this guy! I had to be mature. I replied:

leah,

good call. i don't think we'll have a problem. what are you doing tonight? want to come over and watch tv or something?

-gabe

Call me romantic. Leah replied to accept my invitation and countered with a suggestion that we add that silly kung-fu cooking show to our plans. (Incidentally, I believe this was the moment that our threesome with food actually began.) I left work a little early to shove things in the closet, wipe down surfaces, and make myself look comfortably unprepared. At the time I lived in the kind of apartment building that has a parking lot. It was in South Austin, 78704. Shady and slow and on the Green Belt, old trees and a pool that was supposed to look like a swimming hole with a deck built around it. My apartment was grossly overpriced and coarsely furnished, so I did my best by lowering the lights and uncorking some cheap wine. I was expecting nothing more than a nice evening of sipping table wine from mugs and enjoying a little basic cable. (With the distinct possibility of arm wresting or some other light-contact sport.) By eight I was in my loungin' around and impressin' the ladies pants (egg on the knee) and a clean tee. I had showered but thoroughly dried and tousled my hair so as not to look . . . showered. I assumed my position on the edge of the white kitchen counter opposite the window and next to the fridge, wine in hand, bottle half-empty (maybe half-full), my nerves on another edge altogether.

She drove up, parked ten yards away from my door.

After a brief internal discussion (vendetta) over whether I should open the door while she approached or coolly wait for the anticipated knock, I realized I was standing in the middle of the living room, wine on my shirt, listening to the second round of knocks on the door. "Hey." I greeted her. "Hey." She said "hey" I poured wine and she said something about her landlady, threw her coat on my second-hand orange lounger, and collapsed on the futon. We did go through the motions of spending a boring evening in front of the TV, appropriately distant from each other but just intimate enough that I will never let any woman I'm fond of sit on a couch with another guy. After the video games, after the cooking show, after two bottles of wine she decided that I ought to learn how to leg wrestle. The rest of the evening was spent on our backs, chasing each other around on our hands and knees. You might call it foreshadowing.

I was hungry but she had eaten. She graciously insisted that we go somewhere so I could eat. We ended up at a nearby family restaurant, the type with junk on the walls, the type of place in which Leah would only be caught dead. I had a burger, fries, Coke; she had mediocre apple pie with limp crust. That was our first meal alone, after business hours. Many of the signifi-

cant or arguably significant events that she and I have shared have been impressively unimpressive.

A few days after Leah got in her black Civic hatchback and left my apartment she called me after work, after dark. I was on the phone with a friend, confessing that "Yes, I have some feelings for Leah,'" but insisting that "No, I'm not going to do anything stupid." I clicked over.

"Hello?"

"I broke up with him."

It was Leah. Act surprised.

"Holy shit!"

I could have done better than "holy shit." She continued.

"He came over for dinner and he kept asking what was wrong. He asked if I wanted to break up and I said yes. Then he left."

"Are you sure that's what you want?"

That was much better than "holy shit."

"I don't know. Will you come over and talk to me?"

She didn't seem to notice the very long pause that followed on my end of the line. Eventually — because they always do — the pause ended.

"Okay. Let me get dressed."

She hung up the phone. I didn't actually need to get dressed, but I brushed my teeth for too long and thought about why I was so riled up. I'd been invited out on late-night rendezvous before. Not scores of them, but enough. I'd had crushes before, been rebound before. It's not as clear when you really like someone, though; worse yet when you may be falling in love with her. We had kicked off our friendship by having fun together; always of the mindless sort, conversation never too heavy. At some point, though, things got heavy. On my chest. I kept trying to convince myself that it was just a crush. Well if it's just a crush then why am I still brushing my teeth? I asked myself. Pull yourself together, jerk.

I was getting angry with myself now. This is the point where the cynical reader might wonder, Is this crap really true? And if so, who cares? And if so, who remembers this shit so lucidly? I do. It's my story. Shut up.

I got in my car, opened all the windows, played something loud and drove a cautious seventy miles per hour up Lamar Boulevard and through Leah's neighborhood to her small apartment on South Fifth. The single, narrow visitor's parking spot was providentially available, which meant that I wouldn't have to move my car any time soon. I approached her door and heard some sad record on the other side. Let's say Red House Painters. Thank God it wasn't a song about an ex or lost opportunities. It was a song about a cat, but a sad one, and Leah's eyes were puffy and red when she opened the door. We sat on the couch for a while; she went over her conversation with her ex again. Her phone rang, it was him. She took it into the bathroom and turned on some water. I went to the kitchen and looked in the fridge — milk, ketchup, eggs — I decided to call my friend back.

Leah and I ended our respective conversations at the same time and met back on the couch. "We're going to talk about things tomorrow after work," she said. Great. There goes that. They'd done this at least four times before. It's the classic floundering relationship. She continued,

"He thinks that I might be jumping the gun and wants to talk about things. I mean, I don't think I am but I just want to be sure. You know? I don't know what I expect you to say to that but thanks for coming over. I just get scared sometimes and start doubting myself. Maybe this is the right thing, maybe we should break up but it's not one of those things you want to rush into, right? I always get freaked out and do things I regret."

So I really was just a pal to talk to. Even at best I was just a possible fling so she could stand being with

her boring, stable relationship for a little longer.
Fantastic.

I wanted to go home. I wanted to go home about as
bad as I wanted to go to bed with her. I said the things
I was supposed to — told her that she'd figure things
out and these things take time and I'll be here to listen
and all that shit. I hated saying it. I felt used, uncool,
unattractive, safe. I was so fucking sick of being the safe
guy. I didn't want girls to open up to me anymore, or use
me to get back at their real boyfriends. I wanted to be a
dangerous guy. I wanted a cigarette hanging from my
lip, a few notches on my bedpost, a tattoo. Leah had a
tattoo. Granted, she got it when everyone was getting
tattooed, but it was still cool. With the exception of but-
terflies, dolphins, small flowers, peace symbols, yin-
yangs, and the like, people with tattoos always look like
they have better sex that you — and more of it, with
more people. I finished my bit about following her heart
(or something like that) and started thinking about
going home. She had other ideas.

"Will you sleep over? Just sleep. Like, it would be
nice to have someone to cuddle with." Me: numb, slack-
jawed, knees gone, mouth dry. Sigh. I gathered my
remaining faculties. "Sure. Yeah. Of course. That
makes sense."

She went in to her room to change, shut off the
lights, and told me that I could come in. She was
wearing a faded yellow t-shirt, inside out, with green
and pink flowered pajama pants. Some sort of silly
Japanese-inspired print. I called them Japants. She
thought I was hilarious. I stripped down to boxer shorts
and climbed into her bed. It was squeaky as hell and
small. Her inexpensive little room was ice cold so she
pulled the covers over me, turned around, and backed
in to me, spoon-style. I rested my arm on her hip,
smelled her hair, and fell asleep.

Apart from a sweetly awkward hug that morning we

didn't really talk the next day but that night she did call. It was off, officially. She had gone over to his apartment and they talked about it. He still wanted to stay together but only if she was really sure of it. She obviously wasn't that sure and they ended it in a sobbing (but no doubt hip) embrace. She asked me to come over again and again I sat next to her on her ratty, yellow couch. She jump started the evening by asking, "You clearly want to kiss me so why don't you just get it over with?" I answered with a breakneck and dead cool "Whahuhooha?" She's a real sick fucker so she added: "I heard you're a great kisser. That when you're twenty-five you'll be great in bed, too." So I kissed her. She said "wow," which is the nicest thing anyone's ever said to me.

It was only days later that I gave Leah virtually no pleasure in what I recall as a sexual conquest less graceful even than sex in the back of a car. It started on my couch with the TV on. There was some flirty cuddling going on which led to some more smooches which led, alarmingly quickly, to my bedroom and my fantastically expensive and comfortable bed. Clothes came off, sex was had. Probably ten minutes start to finish. No "wow" this time, just a "you sort of sweated on my boob."

231941401

My girlfriends past bothers me...a lot.

I don't know why I can't get over it...

709883645

I made a huge mistake today and let her go.

643384850

I've been married for years. As time went on I realized that I preferred women to men. My husband is really cool about (I really love him) and lets me dress him up in my clothes and stuff.

Last year I met this girl who I fell head over heels in love with. She moved in with us and I really needed a commitment from her so I made her marry my husband. She even wore my wedding dress and I was the bridesmaid. Of course it's not legal but she doesn't realize that.

Now I mess about with her contraceptives because I want my husband to get her pregnant — mainly because the idea of her all huge and full of a baby really turns me on. I love watching her with my husband as well.

503899487

I was already scheduled to visit a few of my friends at a popular university two hours from here last weekend when this guy I'm dating pissed me off. When my friends and I wont out Saturday night, we all got drunk and I wound up making out with some random guy. I even made a haiku about it:

Boy back home won't know.

Why not mako out with this guy?

I think his name's Rob.

791414137

I'm crazy about this guy who lives upstairs but he's a freak who hates women and likes kung fu.

But he does this really cool thing with his eyebrow.

906969746

I just spent an entire hour of my time looking at 165 pages of girls on Friendster trying to find a picture of the girl he left me for.

It didn't even fucking work.

I'm a complete moron.

I can't sleep or eat and talking to you causes me so much pain its all I can do to keep my eyes open. But not talking to you hurts so much more. I fucking need you and she doesn't. I will fucking love you and she won't. You're throwing us away for the most insane thing in the world. But I still love you and I know that as absolutely fucking pathetic as it is of me, I would get back with you in a second if you wanted when it doesn't work out with her. I've never loved anyone before you, and I don't fucking **want** to love anyone else. When you see me again I'm going to look amazing and I know you won't care but I'm going to look amazing. I've never felt this used in my life. I don't fucking understand and its making me want to die. But I want you to be happy so I'm going to be your friend and I will pick up the pieces when she breaks your heart. I fucking love you so I'm letting you go.

181530915

My almost boyfriend (love for 4 years...too long distance to commit) has had two one night stands in a month. It's not violating the terms of our relationship. But it feels like shit. He says both times he was drunk and was thinking about me the whole time. I really love him. But this really hurts me. I woke up next to him this morning and cried.

685854183

I started eating with my left hand (even though I am right-handed) just because the guy I like is left-handed.

445051592

My girlfriend broke up with me so that she could hook up with her ex. I hated her so much and yet I got back together with her only so I could break up with her and win the relationship. It's been over a year and we're still going out.

309441809

I pretend that I'm in love with my boyfriend, but really I just want him around because he's like the father I never had. He takes care of me and treats me like I'm way younger than him, even though I'm 8 months older. I deliberately don't do any housework so he will tell me what to do and boss me around. I want him to be more dominant in our relationship. The only time I enjoyed having sex with him was this one time when he tied me up, because he had full power over me.

This all sounds a little fucked up, hey?

946939179

I have spent the last three nights spooning and holding hands with a very beautiful, intelligent woman — in her bed. Since she is so attractive, I was too insecure to make a serious move on her while spooning. Now she only refers to me as "her buddy." I missed the chance of my lifetime. I love her. I blew it. Life sucks.

405539053

I used to be a looks fascist, meaning I would only date

guys who were better looking than at least 90% of the population. I got a big charge out of being with hot guys. Most of these guys treated me like shit, and I let them, just so I could think, "Hey look who I'm banging!"

The only exception was for someone semi-famous. He treated me even worse.

Now I'd give anything for an ordinary, normal guy to love me. None of these men ever did. I'd seriously give anything for a good man's love, even if he isn't handsome.

I'm having a really hard time finding that. I hope I will someday.

Guess some people have to learn the hard way.

663670220

My life is messed up. Too many bad things happened to me — yet I am the only one to blame.

I'm in love, but not loved back. Drives me insane, but there is nothing I could do.

One could call it messed up at Beijing.

326590853

Another day.

Love is hard to find.

Every day I feel sadder.

Xylophones are my only friend.

Boobies I have not seen.

Relief I have not felt.

As if that wasn't sad enough.

Kissing isn't my thing.

589298982

I miss the Sierra Mist I left on the bus more than I miss my boyfriend.

206921358

I'm in a relationship that has no passion whatsoever. I can't stand it. If he kissed me with passion, maybe I would give him more interest. No matter how much I want to...I just can't have intercourse with him anymore. I find it gross. It's going on 2 yrs living with him. I look at other guys and talk to others on the phone. I want to leave, but I don't know how. I'm trapped cuz if I did, where would I go?

354360234

Two years ago I was in a great relationship with a girl who just started out as a friend. I've never been closer to another person in my life. She broke up with me after we'd been going out for a little while.

Two months later she came back to me after being away all summer and said it was because she was scared of how close she was getting to me. We started to hang out a bit again. Later we started to go out again.

I told myself and her that I forgave her for how she just suddenly dumped me and didn't speak to me for those two months we didn't speak. I truly hadn't gotten over it though, and after a few months I broke up with her. I haven't talked to her since.

It took me a while, and then it just hit me like a brick in the face. I did the exact same thing she did to me. I don't have the guts to just show up at where she lives or phone her up now. I mean what right do I have to after almost 2 years of not speaking. She lives just around the corner from my house too. She'd probably think I'm crazy if I called her up now, I bet she doesn't think about me anymore even.

The big problem is, I still love her. She was my best friend. I think she was my soul mate, and I let her go.

I can't summon up the guts to contact her. Although I know if something bad happened to her, and I never told her how I felt. I'd probably go crazy.

I miss you LH.

999220523

I'm 21 and in love with a much younger girl. I used to baby sit her when she was just a baby and I've known her her whole life. I feel completely attached to this girl, as our families are very close as well. I wish to marry her one day, but I'm not sure exactly how she feels because she's so young still. I know deep inside that I'll always wait for her though. Sometimes I feel guilty for putting so much on a little girl, but other times I feel that she should feel good because someone loves her so deeply. Even though I do have sexual feelings for her, the romantic and loving feelings are so much more. She's 10.

410951085

I duped the girl I like into going on a luxury holiday with me by telling her I won it on the Internet — she agreed but her boyfriend was angry.

We are good friends and I wanted to spend time with her alone so I paid for the whole trip.

When I got back I told her I had to go away on business and could be in danger. I wrote her a secret note and said she should only open if I died.

I wasn't really going anywhere — I just wanted to see if she would be worried about me and get a hug.

138331968

I have always attracted very charming but dangerous men, and for many years I have decided to live celibate rather than risking again. The most depressing was marrying one of them cos I felt I had no escape. The most painful one was deciding to abort the baby of a psycho...and the guilt for the rest of my life when one charming boyfriend killed a man. The man who died was also a violent person who attacked me, but I don't believe in this sort of justice and will carry that man's death on my shoulders forever.

181232763

I'm a gay teenager and I've got a huge crush on a straight guy who I've known for years. But now both his friends and myself are starting to suspect that he might be gay, also. I'm not sure how to broach the subject when I see him next so I think I'm just going to kiss him.

720965321

I saw some construction workers during my lunch break yesterday. I almost stopped my car. I wanted to get out of my car, drop my pants and lay on the pavement and just tell them to "tear it up."

577281454

I am going to kill myself if I don't get a serious boyfriend by the time I'm 33. I am serious.

I'm 29 now, and I've had sex but never with someone who loved me back. It seems like everyone else falls in love for the first time in high school, maybe college at the latest.

I'm a decent looking woman who went to Columbia University for graduate school and I had no luck finding a boyfriend there either.

I've been told that I give especially good blowjobs by some guys who had gotten them from more women than they could count or remember, so I don't think the issue is poor-quality sex.

Hell, it's not sex at all — I haven't even been kissed or asked out on a date since I was 26.

I'd ask guys out, but all the men around me are attached. And I mean every single goddamn place I go, they all have long-term serious relationships with other women. If by chance they are single, they want something totally casual, which I've done before — it's getting old. I'm getting old.

I keep trying to figure out what other women are doing that I'm not or which qualities I lack that men want.

And I think that since I'm getting close to 30 it is now socially acceptable for me to be tired of that crap.

Freud couldn't figure out what women wanted. Hah. What the hell do men want?

It's killing me that I still don't know what being in love is like. I'm starting to be afraid that I never will.

If I had a man in my life, I'd be so grateful and loving and would never ever cheat, unlike all the people posting on this site. I can't fathom doing that to someone — don't these people realize how lucky they are?

I've already started stockpiling some pills for if/when I'm going to bump myself off.

It is entirely possible to die of loneliness. Believe it.

185137406

I claim that I don't want to get married, but I still get all choked up at weddings, and even wedding scenes in movies, and recently, just looking at photos of a friend's wedding.

281224229

I let her go.

342333053

I've never loved a girl without simultaneously hating her. It's weird, but the more I love her the more I think she's a piece of crap.

743194657

I feel like throwing up when I kiss my girlfriend.

I almost did last night.

562569814

I'm in love with a girl and I am a girl. First time for everything. Life sucks.

484193081

I'm in love with one of my best friends.

Sorry if it's a bit of a cliché.

She's had a long-term serious boyfriend as long as I've known her, and I've always accepted this – she loves him and he always seemed like a decent guy. And at the end of the day, her happiness is what counts.

Despite this, over the last year or so we've got closer and closer, with lots of hugging and lots of big deep talks and stuff like that. And all the time I was getting more and more into her and it was getting harder and harder not to make it obvious and make things uncomfortable (I think if I was being honest, I probably failed – she's not stupid).

Anyway, recently things have changed and this guy is becoming a real asshole to her and he's moving away for a job in about six months, leaving her behind. She's getting more and more miserable and yet she still loves him and there's nothing I can say to her without hurting her.

A (male) friend of mine says that I should just make a move but I'm terrified of fucking up our friendship, which means the world to me. And, just as significantly, whether he's a scumbag or not, you just don't hit on another guy's missus. It's not cricket and all that.

And, if I was being honest, fear of rejection probably has a lot to do with it as well.

So, at the end of the day, here I am – there's a girl who I adore, who I get on great with and who I'd do anything for, and she's in a world of pain thanks to her asshole boyfriend, and there's not much I can do about it (well there probably is, but I'm too much of a pussy).

I'm being far too British about this. Perhaps I should just get her drunk and go from there.

317359716

I don't know if you will ever stumble upon this but I wanted to let my feelings out without being totally vulnerable. I hardly tell you how I feel about you because there is that small fear of rejection. I wanted you to know that I love you more than I have loved any other person in my entire life. I think you are a wonderful person inside and out. I think about you all the time and miss you dearly when we are not together. I really do want to marry you someday and maybe even have your children and I hope that you want the same with me. I hope you read this and know that this is for you. I love you!

520836267

I had the password to my ex-girlfriends email account and read her email through the break-up and for probably a year after. I really shouldn't have but it became an obsession, I had to force myself to quit because it wasn't helping me get over her, I think I still love her, the bitch.

180766939

I wish my loving, caring, honest boyfriend would just fuck off.

191108508

I really am not attracted to my girlfriend anymore. I stay with her because of the dog.

553571955

I befriended this girl who sits on the bus I take to work every morning. I thought she was about 15 or 16, and so it turned out she was 15. She has 1 eye missing and isn't what anyone would consider "attractive" and doesn't really have any friends, but she's a really nice person deep down. I was going out with a drop dead gorgeous girl at the time, I was only with her for her looks, I was a really shallow person. Anyway, this girl I met, we got really close and we stopped at each others houses quite often staying up late watching movies etc. We were the bestest of friends.

1 night we were cuddled up on the sofa watching a romantic type film. I was stroking her hair, but there was a really romantic part in the film where the leading roles were kissing, we both looked at each other, and she said "I love you" so we kissed for ages, it felt so right. 1 thing lead to another and we were making love. It was better than anything I ever experienced. We both pressed exactly the right buttons with each other, and it was heaven. Can't describe the feeling, I knew she was a virgin and had never even held hands with a guy before, let alone kissed one. We stayed up all night kissing and cuddling.

In the morning, I asked her if she really did love me and

she said yes, then asked me what I wanted to do... I told her I loved her too and phoned up my girlfriend telling her all about it and said we were over.

My now (ex)girlfriend is absolutely furious and feels humiliated, cos I left her for an ugly girl with 1 eye, and everyone takes the piss out of her for losing me to this girl.

But I don't care cos I found true love. I know there's an age gap but were perfect together, so I don't care.

Anyone who goes with someone for their looks is stupid. Try talking to someone who looks like they need a friend, you'll be surprised at what they have to offer and how nice they are.

685321066

The basis of my relationship with my boyfriend is giggling and having sex.

497091809

I read my boyfriend's ultra, ultra private journal. Then I went through his personal files and found old letters from his big time serious ex and it makes me feel like he's not over her. This kills me. He just got a letter from her today (I'm apt sitting) and I actually considered throwing it away so he wouldn't ever see it. I fucking hate jealously. Can't I just love someone without a past?

349509778

I finally have a confession — I love this site and come here often. I have always dated computer geeks — relatively good looking guys who I later found out to like computers and spend a little too much time with them.

Right now I'm in a long distance relationship with a wonderful, cute, Microsoft guy. I'm an Apple girl and all can agree I'm no where near ugly, many of my friends and ex's call me the best looking geek ever. The thing is, I never knew this was a deep thing until I saw "the core," I totally wanted to kiss the geek, he totally impressed me, he was the hero of the movie in my eyes.

So my confession is that all you sweet adorable 20+ year old computer geek guys who are still virgins, you're my créme. I love u.

377585419

My life is much better. Without my ex-boyfriend in my life, it's a lot more peaceful, and I'm sure he thinks I miss talking to him, yet I don't. He may read this, hope he does. I hope it makes him feel bad, cause I'm okay without talking to him, and worrying about getting online and having him stalk me. Yeah, life is better without some of your ex's, trust me.

832879743

I went out with a guy just for sex. He was madly in love with me and I was just on for the ride. I dumped him and went for other guys. He slits his wrists now.

464896768

I am still in love with my ex girlfriend from 5 years ago. We still email each other and stuff but I don't have the guts to tell her I still love her. She was one of the biggest influences in my life and I don't think I will ever stop loving her. I would marry her in an instant if I could. She is my soul mate.

194080610

I've developed strong feelings for the singer in an Industrial "Experimental" band. He has a life partner but she's less attractive than me and has a huge forehead. Everyone I know hates him but I find his arrogant, narcissistic behavior a huge turn on. I listen to his tracks naked in my house and long for the day he notices me in those big empty rooms.

886594401

Living well is the best revenge. I'm glad I didn't seek vengeance against any of my old girlfriends. Nothing I could have dreamed up can compare to the mess their lives have become. Take my advice. Take the High Road.

989846938

I can only write good lyrics about my ex-girlfriend. That sucks because I really like my actual girlfriend.

880163330

I'm 18 and male, and I have been sleeping with my best friend's father for four years. He even married my mom just to be with me every chance he could get. I'm better at giving head than her.

202355594

I like boys and I am a boy. His name was Kory. He was a tough one. No one knew until I had the craving for him in the mall. IT could not be held back so I undressed Kory in front of everybody. After 2 years of our relationship we got married then we found out that we were related.

307361202

I spent $60 on jeans yesterday because the sales guy was cute.

457124449

I still think of my ex-wife's boobies.

570164166

I wish I could find the nerve to ask her out.

Finding out her name would be a start.

39623230

I am in love with someone I can't be with, and I'm with someone I can't love.

While traveling by air, alone, meeting other layover people seems unavoidable. More so during the holidays.
They will ask your name, origin and destination, and
what you do — usually in that order. Formalities aside,
and assuming you are both stranded for an indefinite
period with little more than a $10 meal voucher from the
airline (if you're lucky), they will offer to buy you a drink.
To be less abstract: this has happened — without exag-
geration — every time I've traveled alone around the holidays. Fresh off a late inbound flight and waiting to be
reassigned from the connection I missed, I crossed the
terminal to one of those awful airport sports bars. The
edges of the tarmac were being held down on all sides by
eight feet of powder. Inside, the infinite delays, misinfor-
mation, and looping Christmas tunes tape was taking its
toll on the post-holiday crowd of middle-class families,
jet-setting retired couples, and students with their own
pillows. I was only halfway through a long drink when a
shortish guy with no visible luggage extended his hand. I
knew I'd be drinking for free for the next couple of hours.
Flights kept arriving, with very few leaving, so things got
cozy in the only bar in Terminal B. A blond kid in his
mid-twenties and a vacationing flight attendant filled the
empty seats at our table, handshakes all around, and the
generous guy offered another round for the table. I
enjoyed not sitting alone, but I wasn't looking to make
new friends. The kid and the flight attendant were working hard on a tentative New Year's Eve hook-up strategy
while hardly speaking to our benefactor aside from drink

orders. Before an announcement on the intercom peeled me off from the group, the guy with the tab confided that he wasn't even traveling. That he lived near the airport and came here to meet people. The beer in my gut suddenly sat heavy. I wanted to give him a Christmas card or tell him that I'd get him next time. I'd spent most of the past two hours looking in to my glass or fiddling with my cell phone, avoiding his conversation. Three days after Christmas the man with no luggage was just there for some company and all I offered was to greedily drink his hospitality.

514419639

I have, over the course of my life, used several women just for oral sex. When I was 16, I convinced this girl with little self-esteem to give me head. It got to the point where I'd call her at 11 PM and she'd drive to my house to suck me off and then leave again. I continued that, on and off, for four years. Even when I had girlfriends, I'd still call the first girl to come over when no one was around.

She eventually developed feelings for me, but I never used her for anything more than blowjobs. I soon broke off contact with her, and haven't spoken to her in two years. I ran into her the other day, as she now works in one of my movie stores. I talked to her briefly, exchanged pleasantries, and got my movies. She had a longing look in her eyes the whole time. I know I hurt her in the past... but I honestly wanted nothing more than to take her in the back of the store and make her go down on me.

620978978

I've been calling telephone chat lines and wasted 50% of my disposable income. I've done this for twenty years. Cigarettes and hookers take most of the rest. I am a stinky lump of poo-poo but I am trying to change by using this site.

My parents taught me I was useless and I have largely lived up to their expectations

264606956

My friend and I had some weed but no paper to roll a joint with, so we used the page from my Bible that had John 3:16 in it.

I'm going to hell for that.

627236000

When I was in college, I met a girl through an online dating service. We started talking over the phone and she told me she was in love with me.

She flew about 800 miles to visit me. I wasn't really attracted to her, but I had sex with her anyway, because I wanted to see what it was like (I was a virgin).

After she flew home I stopped calling her.

333692089

I start drinking alone at home at 6 PM every Friday evening and before I know it it's Monday again and I have to go to work. I lie to all my coworkers, making up stories about how I go out with ladies and whatnot, but really I guess I'm just a sad lonely alcoholic.

882091369

About two years ago when I was 20, at a student union conference I decided to destroy my internal organs through a combination of:

a) Whiskey
b) Pot
c) Speed

There were several outcomes of this potent cocktail of doom. Firstly, I ended up shagging some fairly average girl at an after-party, who I'd smutted a few evenings before. The amusing thing was that we didn't have any condoms and I'd left my wallet somewhere. I made her pay for the taxi to drive to the 7/11, pay for the condoms, and then pay for the taxi back to the party.

We then proceeded to bonk on the nearest lawn. It was fairly satisfying, although I think I spoiled the moment by joking I had herpes. However I was in a drunken mood for mischief, which culminated in my draping the used condom on the door handle of an Anglican church.

That isn't the end of it. This girl left the party and went home, and 10 minutes later another lady was sitting in my lap. Being the foul-mouthed yobbo I am, I told her every detail of what I'd done over the last half an hour. She had a boyfriend, but was so impressed by my decadent behaviour that she ended up giving me a hand job, and, wait for it, went and retrieved the used condom and put it in the bin.

My fellow student representatives thought I was insane.

618001938

I get friends addicted to cocaine so I can have someone to share my misery.

930179675

This one time I was on a bus and the trip took about 16 hours. I really didn't have enough space, and it wasn't comfortable at all.

So after a while some girl came to sit next to me, and we started talking about lots of crap. And I noticed she had this really comfy pillow.

So in the middle of the night I woke up and I saw we were holding hands. And she was just starring at me. So we started kissing a bit and making out. We were busy for 2 hours or something like that. And no 1 in the bus noticed. Then I told her I'm really tired and I need some sleep, so she gave me her pillow and I put my head on her lap. All I cared for was the damn pillow.

In the end she asked me: "How old are you anyway?" "18"...she looked at me like WTF? So I asked, "How old are you?" "24." After that she gave me her number but I never planned to call her back. She was cute, but she shouldn't start making out on a bus with a total stranger, even if it was with me.

I don't feel bad about using her at all, she asked for it.

194206869

I fucked up the rent money this month buying heroin, porn, and a slew of anal beads and vibrators. Now I have to take one of those short-term high interest loans online just so I won't be evicted. I am so damn stupid I really don't deserve to have my own place.

920215928

I'm a good little girl from a nice Catholic home, with

bulimia and ADD and a drinking problem and a predilection for smooth-talking womanizers with drug habits.

539413826

Marijuana saved my life. While high, I learned what it felt like to not obsess over things, to be free of the fears of rejection and abandonment, and what it was like to feel sexually powerful. I was able to take that sense of normality back into my waking life, and everything changed because of it. Now I kind of like my job, I'm making new friends, and I have a girlfriend who loves me very much.

This is a confession because it's something I feel people should know about me, but at the same time, I don't want them to know it's *me*. I'm not particularly proud of it because I needed something external to become a whole person. I still have to get high about once every other week to remind myself how I want to be.

150636360

Sometimes I eat so many Skittles, and I eat them so fast that I lacerate my gums. I'll go to brush my teeth afterwards but I have to stop because all this blood is pouring out of my mouth. Also I get a bad stomach ache and I have crazycrazycrazy dreams. I have another pack of Skittles in my pocket and I'm going to go eat them right now.

313217326

I love porno like a fat kid loves cake.

376989132

I may pretend to be interested in someone's religion just to make out with them.

881221462

I often say derogatory things about people and then hang out with them and let them buy me beers hours later.

50934713

I wish I hadn't messed up the many friendships I once had. And I wish pain wasn't such a casual companion to love, and that love really was blind instead of dumb. And I wish I never hurt him just because he hurt me. I wish I was a better person in that way.

602883989

I joined a multi-level marketing scheme and then realized that I'd have to push it on all of my friends, relatives, and anyone else I came in contact with.

I decided I don't want to sell them all out like that and don't want to be "that multi-level marketing guy."

So now I have a license that cost a few hundred $ to sell a multi-level product and haven't used it once.

420023216

I'm 17 and still a virgin. I could have sex if I wanted to but I don't know if I do. I've had oral sex before and it wasn't too fun.

My sister drinks cheap alcohol.

966352329

When no one is looking, I eat the pineapples at work. I love the pineapples. It's not like many people order pineapples on their pizza anyway. I also eat the pepperonis...lots of pepperonis.

294641101

I seem to do about 10 - 20 diddlers a week, about half a g of coke and drink shit loads, usually topped off with a quarter of the finest ganesh. I like to get fucked out of my tits all the time and it seems that my heart has started missing beats and I also keep getting these electric shocks all over my body and it feels like my brain is hemorrhaging. My nose is rotting away and I have the shits like nobody could imagine. I think I'm going to die soon. Don't do it.

856247335

I secretly still am addicted to Hanson, even though I'm a hardcore emo kid.

276071887

On New Years Eve, I got really drunk and crashed at my friend's place, and so did my other friend who is a guy, and his boyfriend. They're gay. I'm a guy. In the middle of the night, his boyfriend came in my bedroom and we made out. I liked it. A lot. And I tell people I'm straight.

533852213

Yesterday I ate a whole pizza.

691183065

Today I ate a 20-piece box of McNuggets by myself. I'm on Atkins, and I didn't think the breading would add that many carbs. I thought wrong. I ate 72 grams of carbs today instead of 20. It's nothing but salad and chicken for the rest of the week.

503868058

I feel sick when I think about the abuse I have done to my body. E.g., one night I was at a rave, and I had eaten, snorted, swallowed, and pinged the alphabet, and was loving the lights, and sounds, and people. Cranking hard on the dance floor then all of a sudden I'm in hospital with the lights searing my eyes, doctors and nurses screaming my name. I just turned my head, threw up, and passed out again. Woke up covered in drips and heart monitors (heart was at 150 at one stage), the nurse wanted my parent's number but I had turned 18 the week before, and just gave my g/f's mobile. She turned up and I snuck out. Once I had strength to walk, I went back to the rave. Dropped another lollie and finished my night out. Looking back I can't believe how stupid I was.

633914047

One time I waited until my g/f went to sleep, then I took her car and money and bought heroin with it. On the way back I nodded off from the dope and wrecked her car. I lied and said I got ran off the road. I'm a dirt bag.

340567890

It's 7:30 AM right now. I've been drinking and doing coke all night. I have to be at work in an hour.

As I'm sure you've guessed I'm calling in sick this morning and sleeping off one of the worst hangovers of my life.

361673160

I need to get this out. Years ago I took LSD with a good friend. I ended up thinking he was a space alien and beating [him] up with a baseball bat, which I thought was like a Star Wars light sabre. He ended up in the ER and took another three weeks in hospital to recover. It freaked me out and I never had the courage to tell him it was me.

441423750

I eat, and eat, and eat, and eat, and it seems that I never get full. I am hungry all the time. I just got done going into the kitchen at 5:00 in the morn, proceeded to — brace yourselves now — eat my mom's homemade beef stew OUT of the crock pot with my bare hand. And here I am trying to lose weight. Even I make myself sick. That has to be one of the most vile things I've ever done. I'd most likely be bulimic if throwing up my stomach content didn't bother me as much as it does...sorry you had to read that people.

269994052

About 8 years ago, I helped this girl I sort of knew shoot heroin for her first time. Actually, she just held out her arm and I injected it for her. She said she was going to do it herself if I didn't help her, and she didn't know how, so I did it to keep her from doing it wrong and injecting air or just generally making a mess of her arm. So, I could sort of rationalize it at the time; besides, me and all my friends were doing it pretty regularly then.

Not too long after that she became a stripper. And about three years later I saw her at a restaurant with a much older businessman-type guy. She looked like she was still strung out and I can't shake the feeling that she was probably working as a hooker.

I haven't done heroin for about 6 years. I don't know what happened to her.

469666749

I normally do not smoke but when I am really stressed out about something, I can comfortably smoke nearly a pack a day.

658507542

My roommates leave their clothes lying on the bathroom floor a lot, and we often run out of towels. So sometimes, when I don't have a towel and don't have time to air dry...I use their clothes to dry myself off.

380172758

I can't socialize without being drunk. Everybody knows this about me though. Maybe it's not a confession.

518101173

I am 20 years old. I have slept with 21 guys and 3 girls. I have never been tested. I am too afraid that I have something. Five of those people were in a 3 month span, and I never told my boyfriend (whom I did not sleep with) about any of them. During that time I was eating E twice a week. I ended up rolling* every weekend for a year and a half. I quit cold turkey and have only taken it twice since then. I have only slept with 3 people in the past two years. But now I started eating shrooms and I cheated on my girlfriend last weekend while on shrooms.

I know that I am not as slutty when I do not take drugs.

But I think that I use drugs as an excuse to be a slut.

Once at a rave I lied to a guy and said I was rolling so I could sleep with him.

*Doing Ecstasy (MDMA).

I have stolen change, mints, some office supplies, Jordan almonds, a mouse from a job that laid me off, several cups of coffee, a few beers, a wine glass, salt, a couple of chicken wings, design ideas, and some subway rides.

The last time I hopped a fence for a little forbidden hot tub funtime, the tub had been very recently shock-treated. My girlfriend and I were busted — nude — by a kid in an AJ's Security uniform who didn't blink as we got dressed. She went unaffected but I, for three days, sported a flaky rash with a side of burning hair smell on all my favorite places.

Oh, and there's this library book on my coffee table that was overdue in 1987, but I truly intend to return it.

668016518

Back in college, I had this pal who had a really annoying neighbor. She had this ugly-assed dog she supposedly paid a lot of money for, and all night it would just bark, bark, and bark. My pal had these plans to shoot the dog, but one night we got really stoned and decided to steal the dog and hold it for ransom (you know those pot dreams). We stole the dog, but neglected to say, tell her or leave a note. I kept the dog at my place, and he actually turned out to be a pretty cool little dog. Well, the neighbor called the police, and things got hot an heavy so I sort of had to keep the dog at my place for a while... and then weeks turned into years...

Last week, he died at age 15 (we think). He's lived with me since I was 21, moved across the US twice, and been a loving and devoted pet to my two sons. I told my wife I found him in the street when we were dating and sort of kept up the lie since then.

I have no idea if I did the right thing or not, but I miss my little buddy so much.

197944889

Today I shoplifted a bag, 2 shirts, a dress, a jumper, and 2 pairs of pants. About $500 worth, and a few of the things I am fairly sure I won't even use. I feel guilty about it, but I have done it many times in the past, and I am sure I will do it again. I can't stop now, it's become almost like an illness. It's not that I can't afford to buy what I need to get by — I just don't want to.

866300444

When I was 23 years old, I got drunk, stripped completely naked, and climbed out onto the railing of my townhouse balcony at 3 AM or so. In the townhouse next to mine lived a married couple about fifteen years older than me, and the woman was hot, hot, hot. I assumed correctly that they did not bother to lock their balcony door (neither did I), so I climbed over the dividing wall and then went right into their bedroom. Both of them were naked and asleep on top of the sheets. The husband was snoring so loudly, I could have belched the alphabet and they wouldn't have heard it. I walked around to the lady's side and admired her for a while, then I leaned down and sniffed her skin (and hairy places) as closely as I could. Then, at a loss for what to do next, I simply took one of their pillows and climbed back over to my own balcony. They never knew a thing about it, and we continued for several more years to have polite neighborly relations. I still have that pillow in my bed, as a matter of fact.

600195923

I stole the hubcaps off a friend's car, then blamed another friend when he threatened to press charges, they're both dicks anyhow.

159119340

I work at a local co-op, in the beverage department. A certain soda company was holding a contest that gave a 100 thousand dollar prize. Realizing that the shit job I was working would never give me that kind of cash, I took almost an entire case of the soda. And, in search of the money, took off all the caps without drinking or paying for any of the soda. I just took it to the trash compactor and dumped it. I'm still broke. For shame.

702463450

I have your property and have no intentions of giving it back in one piece. That being said, it is safe to assume that it is in several pieces. That's right, I cut it into several pieces and hid it so no one can find it except me. This is what you get for stealing what was rightfully ours. Payback is a bitch, isn't it?

69369324

When I was 13, I used the free public phone in my church to call 1-900 sex lines, racking up about $80 in calls. They confronted a group of about 20 kids in the church, including me, and when they asked, I denied it. I felt so guilty the next week I put 20 dollars in the offering plate, hoping that would make up for it.

18091785

When I worked at McDonalds, I often gave them hell by spitting in food, using my lighter to burn the buns, and pretending that I could not hear on the drive-thru radio. Sometimes, I would throw boiling hot water into the trash cans so that the plastic would melt and my co-workers would have to clean the hot, wet food off the trash cans.

The worst, however, was when I was bet twenty dollars that a very beautiful girl would not be drinking my man juices by the end of the day. I released my sin into her McFlurry, then put more flurry in it and M&Ms.

Now that I am Manager of this McDonalds, I regret all that I did in the past, except the stealing.

699622873

Once in college my buddies and I got a letter in our mail-box that was addressed to some people down the street. It looked like a card, and we were feeling like jerks, so we steamed it open over a teakettle. It said "Congratulations on Your Marriage. Have a Great Life Together. — Aunt Judy." She also included $200 cash. My buddies and I took the money, and threw away the card. I'm honestly, truly ashamed of myself and it makes me sick to think about it.

847385072

Today, while drinking at happy hour at an undisclosed chain restaurant, a disgruntled psychotic patron threw a bar stool at the bartender. In the shuffle he lost his pre-scription barbiturates. I stole them and just swallowed one. I hope he didn't need those pills to stop him from killing someone.

505190362

Me and 12 friends ran out on a $125 bill at Denny's. We gave that poor waitress hell too.

579148740

I'm going to steal my roommate's Dilbert calendar tonight. I feel sort of bad about doing this, but she has it coming to her.

225185166

I stole about 15 road signs and mailboxes, even important ones like stop signs. People might die because of it, but I don't care because if you can't tell when to stop, you don't deserve to live.

202726686

When I was about 13 my friend and I snuck out of our houses one night and got loaded off cheap vodka I stole from my dad. We roamed the streets yelling at passers by and eventually made our way into one of those Arabian all night convenience stores. With the liquor in us, we were feeling pretty daring and decided to rob the store of several bags of barbeque charcoal. For what purpose, I don't know. So here we are walking around, completely drunk with bags of charcoal and nothing to do...so we start hurling the coal at cars driving by while hiding in some bushes. Eventually we get bored of that and start throwing the entire bags. Well we had some good luck with this for a while, but then we threw one that landed right through the windshield of this shitty old Nissan or some kind of shit car like that. A couple of big African men got out and chased us through the woods. After about 5 minutes of running, both of us were out of breath and the angry black gentlemen caught up with us and thoroughly beat the living shit out of us and stole our money. When my mom woke me up for school the next morning I explained all the bruises by telling her I had fallen down the stairs during the night and accused her of being a bad mother for not hearing it. She felt bad and went out and bought me breakfast from McDonalds, and a VHS copy of *Raiders Of The Lost Ark*. I feel horrible about it in retrospect, but sometimes I'll be sitting in my desk at work and just burst into a maniacal fit of laughter thinking about the incident.

72627526

I used to steal money out of my parents' wallets to buy tapes/CDs, or to buy candy and snacks at school. Just like two or three dollars a day, so they wouldn't notice. They never did notice.

242057155

I have stolen dirty panties. Sometimes they belonged to sisters of friends of mine. Sometimes they belonged to girlfriends of friends. Sometimes they belonged to friends.

785001704

I do receipt scams on local stores. I have made off with almost $1,000 dollars in CDs, books and other fun things. I don't plan on stopping any time soon.

674347478

As a general rule I don't really steal or shoplift, with one exception — I steal water when I'm shopping at a big store like Kmart or Target. I go to the cooler, grab a bottle of water, drink it while I'm shopping, and don't pay for it at the register. I'm not ashamed. I figure, if I don't get the water, I'll be dehydrated and I'll get cranky and leave without buying anything, so it's actually in the store's best interest to provide me with free water.

743213865

Even though I shop at Wal-mart, I hate Wal-mart. Since I hate Wal-mart, I steal from Wal-mart. Every time I shop there, I steal something. I think they deserve it. However, I do return the cart, every time.

597590666

I steal my roommate's Frosted Flakes and chewy bars.

381684486

I stole a grilled cheese sandwich from a catholic school, a rainbow lei off a mannequin at American Eagle, the entryway floor rug to my apartment building, a "slow children" road sign off my street, and a tank top from the thrift store.

927674213

I stole money from the offering plate to buy pornography, and then instead of buying the porn, I stole it. I really didn't care even though the preacher's kids had bad shoes and bad teeth.

465737975

Last month my car broke down at the store, I didn't feel like walking, so I stole one of those handicapped motorized shopping carts and rode it home. Then I sold it on eBay.

813706774

I got fired today because I stole a sandwich for lunch. I'm going to tell everybody I quit. I hated that damn job anyway.

418853682

One time when I was like 13, I found my mom's dildo. I brought it to school and showed all my friends. We used it to hit girls in the back of the head during lunch...we screamed out "Bitch u just got **coldcocked**." So of course we got caught after someone told on us, my mom got called up to the school to collect me and her dong. I was suspended, and grounded, but it was still one of the best moments of my life watching the pure embarrassment as my principal handed my mom a giant rubber penis!!!

710884420

I steal cars for a living. This doesn't bother me, what bothers me is that I have full coverage insurance on the car I drive, it is so not worth it.

310046853

There's a guy at work who keeps candy in a little dish on his desk. Whenever I pass his cubicle and he's not there, I take a handful of that shit.

5121778

I would steal $20 a day from my sister when she would talk shit to me.

371996448

I stole a pair of boxer shorts from my apartment building dryer and wore them around imagining who it was that owned them — was it you? Or was it you?

924136699

I work next to Google, and I always steal their bagels.

961712537

I stole something yesterday from a dollar store.

And bought something else.

I stole a dollar's worth. What is that?

531496909

One time I saw a bum sleeping in the park, and I stole all his cans, and his backpack, and everything, and threw it in the creek that runs through that park.

657135745

Late one night at the college parking lot garage, I found an unlocked car. The owner probably forgot to lock the driver's door. It was towards the end of the semester, so people had a lot of clothing and room stuff in their cars that night. I jacked everything in that car: his entire wardrobe (at least what fit), cordless phone, CD player, even all his books and backpack, and put it in my car. The next day, I hear the owner walk past his car and say to his buddy that he left the doors unlocked and everything got jacked, and I was right behind him.

I also easily broke into a CRX and took the CD deck to replace the CD deck on my car, which got stolen the month before.

And I don't feel guilty. :)

absolution

*"It is the confession, not the priest,
that give us absolution."*

— OSCAR WILDE

In January 2004 the BBC* reported that the Vatican does
not consider online confessions to be valid. I agree that
getting something off of your chest on a Web site won't
Wash Away Your Sins any more than talking to a priest
will. In fact, I think I read something in the papers recently suggesting that some priests might be just a little more,
oh, let's say fallible than some of us regular Joes. No, it
turns out that nobody is going to undo anything you've
done. The best we can do is own up to being a wrong now
and again, learn from it, make good with those you hurt,
and move on a little wiser. If talking to a priest makes
your nipples hard, good for you. Or maybe giving your
money to an analyst, counselor, social worker, yogi, or
dead ancestor is your thing. That's cool. Send me $20 and
I'll hit you back with an It's Okay, Buddy, We All Make
Mistakes card with a baby chewing a cat's tail or a couple
of whales breaching or something.

I was forwarded the following saying:

"Many affected by the same evil, is only a consolation for the fool."

*BBC World Service; Sunday, January 25, 2004;
bbc.com/sunday.

I completely agree. The way I remember that saying is, "if everyone else jumped off of a building, would you?" Most of us learned that early on. Mark Twain has another saying:

> Twenty years from now you will be more disappointed by the things that you didn't do than by the ones you did do. So throw off the bowlines. Sail away from the safe harbor. Catch the trade winds in your sails. Explore. Dream. Discover.

And I like that one, too. It's not as easy to figure out, and it doesn't fold in to most religious smoothies quite as well, but it's just as important. If I'd only ever taken my elders's word on everything my whole life, I never would have gotten a ticket, had my heart broken, thrown up in a taxi, been in a fight, or lost at gambling. I also never would have smoked a joint, gotten lost in Mexico, fingered a girl, landed a job that I wasn't qualified for, or stolen into an off-limits hot tub. Sometimes you try something dangerous because you really want to; sometimes you do it just because it scares you; sometimes you think it will make you better; and on occasion you may actually do it to feel worse, for sympathy or maybe just an excuse to drink during the day.

Confession happens when you have a big healthy fight, tell the ugly truth, when "I love you" first trips off your tongue. It's not sacred, or some tenet of morality that needs to be directed by rich men. It's visceral, you want to do it.

Some Email

A few emails I've received, to give you the flavor of the various responses to grouphug.us:

You've now denied two completely valid confessions of mine. They didn't break any rules. They were spelt an punctuated properly
Grrr

I am simply writing you to congratulate you on the ingenious idea you have for a website. You have single handedly broken down the laws of decency with the help of modern communication technology, and I think that the result is a forebrearer (sic) of the future world of human communications. I think that modesty and taboos will become irrelevant once people realize the vast range of human depravity that exists throughout society, that which your website illustrates. I do not think you realize the importance of your innovation. Someday historians will reflect on this day and age, and conclude that your simple programmings (sic) were some of the most important unintentional documents of civilization. A la the writings of Soicrates (sic). Furthermore, your website is entertaining in a most deep and fulfilling fashion. Thank you once again, and keep up the good work. I envy you.

[name removed]

I do love what you've done, but that isn't the reason. I sent a confession in, number [removed], and I really need to retract it. Can you send me a confirmation saying you have removed it? I need my girlfriend, the roof over my head and the peace of mind. Thank you thank you, when you come back in the next life you will all be, I don't know what but it'll be great. God or something.

[name removed]

A truly inspired idea constituting part of the 0.00000001% of good things that appear on the web.
I made up that statistic. Statistically less than 1% of statistics are accurate.
It's a great site.

[name removed]

The word confession has some religious connotation because of the Sacrament of the same name. For non-religious persons who are not looking for God's pardon, maybe this site is beneficial because they can let out of their chest things that make then unhappy. It is what we do by going to a Psychologist. By reading the confessions of others they may realize that they are not the worse sinners in the world (even though we don't have to be "thee" worse to go to hell), and this might make their burden lighter. However, there is a saying that goes: "many affected by the same evil, is only a consolation for the fool". But if they are lead to believe that allowing the whole world to know their secret faults, they don't have to worry about them anymore, then this site is detrimental, because the only way to get rid of our sins: REPENTANCE and AMENDMENT.
What I don't understand is the existence of this site

per se. If you don't charge, nor sell lists of valid e-mail addresses, nor begin bombarding us with spam advertising God knows what for depression or sexual products or porno, how do you pay the expenses or get a benefit by reading all the miseries of the souls? If at least you had an experience counselor and replied to your selected sinners, I could see a redeeming value. (By the way I got into this site by accident and would appreciate not to receive spam in my e-mail address).

[name removed]

I used to think you rocked. You had confessions that seemed to mean something but, now I think you suck.

Your current confessions are overheated and lame, they all seem to be written by titillated teans (sic) with too much time . . . the self moderation factor doesn't seem to be working very well.

That said, I love the idea. Good luck.

[name removed]

Well ooookay then.

First off, this site rocks. it's like going to the church and sitting in that little box, but having to leave the comforts of your own home.

Second off, I happened to send in an entry I'd rather not have published. (if it was even considered. In a drunken state, I happened to tell my roommate about how cool this site was and that he should try it out, and that I certainly had.

It slipped my mind that that entailed him visitting (sic) the site, and reading my confession, which is just not a good thing. And believe me, he won't rest, and he'll know which one is mine. it's the one referring to a "two-room threesome" While I have no qualms him finding out that I jerk off while he has female freinds (sic) over, I have a major problem him finding out that I'm in love with him, which I also foolishly mentioned.

If this entry could be rejected when you read it while weeding out the wheat from the chaff, I would be immensely grateful.

Keep on rocking.

[name removed]

Hey. I just visited your site for the first time this evening. It was amazing. It really puts a lot of things in perspective. I spent almost an hour reading it, and as a writer, I got a lot of great ideas from it. Sometimes it's important to examine humans from different angles.

However, I do feel like you guys as the site sponsors are obligated to at least put some links to helpful hot-lines, like those for sexually assaulted/rape victims, or alcoholics, or drug addicts or suicidal people.

I respect the anonymity of the site and I appreciate it.

Yet, I would sleep better at night if you guys had links posted, just an offering to users, but an option that could change lives.

Thanks also for just having this.

We are fucked up, but hopeful.

Love,

Molly

I recently (a few weeks ago) became approved as a moderator for this site, which I used to frequent when it was new. However, after much deliberation, I have found that I cannot in good conscience take part in this venture.

The logic is that, by revealing these confessions to others, even if they are anonymous, is not solving anything. It is simply recounting past sins. If this site is to truly aid people, it must not post the confessions, and thus must not exist as it is. I find it detrimental to my outlook (and to others' outlooks on the world) to recount past transgressions. If, as a mod[erator], I were at the least able to respond to the people who, in their confessions, are seeking help, then I could see merit in aiding this project. As it is, I would quite frankly enjoy seeing this site shut down so that what is done is done and is not brought back to life; however, that is your decision, not mine,and I leave you to make the choice you find to be the true and right choice.

In conclusion, Jesus loves you. =^_^=

Sincerely,

[name removed]